WHY HULK HOGAN MATTERS

ALSO BY DAVID SHOEMAKER

THE SQUARED CIRCLE

WHY HULK HOGAN MATTERS

DAVID SHOEMAKER

THE RINGER

HARPER

An Imprint of HarperCollins*Publishers*

 For information, address HarperCollins Publishers, 195 Broadway, New York, NY 10007. In Europe, HarperCollins Publishers, Macken House, 39/40 Mayor Street Upper, Dublin 1, D01 C9W8, Ireland.

HarperCollins books may be purchased for educational, business, or sales promotional use. For information, please email the Special Markets Department at SPsales@harpercollins.com.

hc.com

FIRST EDITION

Designed by Tai Blanche

Library of Congress Cataloging-in-Publication Data has been applied for.

ISBN 978-0-06-351864-3

Printed in the United States of America

26 27 28 29 30 LBC 5 4 3 2 1

To Dom, Etienne, and Aubrey,
who let me relive all of this
through their eyes.

CONTENTS

INTRODUCTION

I was ten years old, sitting in the Wednesday-night activity room at my church, when the youth group leader gave us the task of retelling a Bible story of our choice in a modern way. My buddy Sean Bailey and I grinned at each other; it didn't take us long to find our muse. He brought in a video camera, I brought in my Hulk Hogan LJN action figure, and our magnum opus was born as *Hulk Hogan as Samson*. I'm not sure that there was much of a narrative device beyond reciting the Samson tale with wrestlers in the main roles, but it worked. Hogan was the strongman of our era, and Samson was a biblical hero worth revising.

Of course, the Samson story is not a tale of pure heroism. It's about how one man, even with otherworldly strength, can be brought to his knees by weakness in morality. It's about the consequences of sin. It's about ego leading a man to ignore his purpose, about the suffering and indignity that caused, and about finding his way once again. It's a story that parallels better today than it did then.

Samson was a much bigger deal in Sunday school than he is in sermons aimed at adults. When I think of him, I immediately go back to childhood, to the way his story felt to me as a kid, and to the idea that morality and belief can make a person into a superhuman. I know now that Samson is a cautionary tale, but hearing the name, I just think of the superhero in the Old Testament, and despite the fact that it's a hollow reading, it still matters. There's a reason they teach about Samson in Sunday school.

And there's a reason why Hulk Hogan, after the collapse of the temple, still matters. This book is that story.

WHY HULK HOGAN MATTERS

CHAPTER 1

THE WANNABE

HULK HOGAN VS. WRESTLING

At 160 North Albany Avenue, a block off Highway 60, the road that cuts across the middle of both Tampa and the state of Florida like a world title belt, there's a white office building that used to be the center of the pro wrestling world for anybody born south of Jacksonville and north of Havana. There was a window in the middle of the storefront under a big hand-painted arrow that read, WRESTLING OFFICE TICKETS and on the plate glass to the left, in front of the white miniblinds, DEEP SOUTH SPORTS INC. This was where it all started.

It was a nice enough building but it wasn't arena-sized by

a long shot, so naming it the Tampa Sportatorium was a bold choice. Cowboy Luttrell, who once got legit knocked out by Jack Dempsey in a boxer-versus-wrestler exhibition, named it that back in the '60s, before he sold the promotion to Eddie Graham. The Sportatorium was the home of not just the Deep South office but also the studio in which Championship Wrestling from Florida (CWF) taped their television show every week and sent it out to the local stations all over the state. For folks watching TV in their living rooms, it was the home of the Brisco Brothers, the Great Malenko, Chief Wahoo McDaniel, the Funks, Hiro Matsuda, Dusty Rhodes, and "Superstar" Billy Graham. (Superstar was the in-storyline "brother" of Eddie, as well as of Dr. Jerry Graham and Luke Graham, all of them bleached blond but none of them actually related.) In early 1977, twenty-three-year-old Terry Bollea walked in. He didn't walk out.

There's a fanciful version of this story where he walks in as Terry Bollea and walks out rechristened as Hulk Hogan, but that's not this story. The truth is probably more fantastic: He didn't walk out because he was carried out, with either a broken leg or something less severe, depending on who you believe, or how much of the retelling has been retrofitted into the pro wrestling mythos.

Perhaps this tale should serve as a disclaimer. There is nothing—nothing—in the world of pro wrestling that you should take as discernible fact unless you witness it with your own eyes, and if what you witness is inside a wrestling ring, obviously toss that aside, too. Pro wrestling is a world of fantasy and fiction, of real athletes performing choreographed stunt work that straddles the line between reality and unreality, and all of that is structured deliberately to evoke a Pavlovian response from the crowd. Even if the viewer knows it's fixed, we are compelled to watch as if it's real. The real world—the wrestler's life backstage and outside the arena—is no less mythological.

In the modern era, as wrestlers have been forced to be honest about the fact that the matches are scripted, kayfabe has subtly shifted to cover the "real life" lore instead of the in-ring product. We know the matches are fixed, sure, but the hell we went through to get there was worse than anything that we pretend in front of crowds. And for his part, Hulk Hogan is not just a legend in the ring but a legendary liar and exaggerator. Just like his on-screen persona, he's a peerless storyteller and a supremely unreliable narrator. Which brings us back to Tampa.

If you started at North Albany Avenue and drove due north from the Sportatorium about nine miles and then hooked a left, you'd be at 5305 North Armenia, which was Doc Castellano's Imperial Room Lounge. That's where the wrestlers hung out on Tuesday nights after the matches at the Fort Homer W. Hesterly Armory. That's where Terry Bollea hung out sometimes, too, because he knew the wrestlers came in every week. He loved going to the matches and he wanted to see the wrestlers in real life, see them at their dark tables, country-and-western music clinking in the background. That's where he met the Brisco Brothers. The Briscos were pro wrestling royalty—Jack was a former NWA world champion and, with his brother Gerry, held tag team championships six times by then, and would hold them another fourteen times before all was said and done.

The Imperial Room is where you could see wrestlers outside of their usual kayfabe pursuits, but the code still stood—heroes on one side of the bar, dastardly heels on the other, groupies roaming freely between the two ends. Bollea had been working out, adding muscle to his enormous, doughy frame. By the age of twelve, Terry had already outgrown most of his teachers. He walked like a kid aware of his own shadow—too long, too heavy. In those days, Tampa was a divided place: equal parts paradise and scrapyard, the new highways running like arteries through neighborhoods that still remembered cattle and sawdust. He played baseball, literally twice the size of the other kids on his team. He played well enough to catch the eyes of scouts for a while, before an arm injury derailed that track. But there was something in the way the crowd's noise folded around him, even in Little League, that he never quite forgot. When he started going to the wrestling shows, he heard the echo of those crowds. He started lifting weights for real in his early twenties, and amid the clang of plates and the smell of iron dust and chalk, he began to rebuild himself into a wrestler. That's who the Briscos saw, standing nervously off to the side at the Imperial Room one night, six and a half feet tall with blond hair to his shoulders. They looked him over and told him he should give wrestling a shot.

Or maybe it happened at The Other Place, where Bollea's band Ruckus played, and the Briscos went to see him there. Or perhaps Hogan pulled aside Mike Graham (wrestler and son of Eddie), whom Bollea knew from high school, and begged him for a shot. Stories differ. In the history of pro wrestling in general and Hulk Hogan in particular, there's no fact too benign to be falsified. But there's mythologizing and then there's self-mythologizing, and the other concept that makes a mess of pro wrestling history is wrestlers' sometime insistence on making themselves the center of the story, whether or not they were. The wrestling term here is "putting yourself over," the same phrase you'd use to describe a self-congratulatory in-ring monologue.

So maybe the Briscos made up their story to make themselves part of Hogan's origin story. Maybe Hogan made it up to be its hero. More than one thing could certainly be true, but in this case it's fair to assume that at least one is a lie. Regardless, the ending was the same: Sure, the Brisco Brothers and/or Mike Graham said to Bollea with a smirk. Sure, kid. Go to the office and ask for Hiro Matsuda.

The Imperial was one thing, but the Deep South office was the place where kayfabe became reality. If you wanted to be a wrestler in Florida, that's where you went. When the cameras were off, the ring that they used to stage the TV show was called the Snake Pit, and the boss of the Pit was Matsuda, the Japanese villain and mainstay of the Florida territory. Matsuda made you do a thousand push-ups and a thousand Hindu squats before you ever got into the ring. Then the real pain started, with Hiro in charge of weeding out the weak at heart with tortuous hooking. The way Hogan told it, Matsuda wrestled in front of crowds six days a week, and he ran the Snake Pit on his only day off, but the truth is Matsuda was mostly retired from the limelight by then. He was still every bit the brute, though. He went hard at the newcomers, practically begging them to give up, to walk away and never come back. There were other tough guys around, too, to make sure you left aching, broken, and positive that wrestling was the realest sport there was. Bob Roop, a heavyweight Greco-Roman wrestler at the 1968 Olympics, twisted the applicants into painful submission. If he was in a bad mood, Eddie Graham would get his licks in, too, and even his friends paint him as borderline psychotic in his treatment of wannabes.

Even if you had an in, like Terry Bollea did, it didn't necessarily go any better. The Briscos must have known what they were sending him into that day. A thousand push-ups, a thousand squats, and then into the ring, under the roughneck tutelage of Matsuda, who craned his neck to look up at the "nice-looking, big boy," determined to see if he really wanted it. In Tampa the air hung thick with salt and petroleum, and there was no air-conditioning or windows in the room, and the Florida heat was amplified by the stage lights. It must have been 115 degrees in there, the kind of heat where Bollea could smell every drink he had the night before sweating out of his forehead. Finally Matsuda welcomed him into the ring. Hiro started in on his head, worked his way down to his arms, and finally wrapped himself around his leg. Matsuda glanced over at Graham, who gave him a nod. He twisted Hogan's ankle until it snapped.

Now, of course there's some dispute as to whether Matsuda actually broke Bollea's leg or whether he just sprained his ankle or pulled a muscle. It stands to reason that the story would be amplified through time, repetition, and kayfabe. Today, Gerry Brisco politely says he "injured his ankle." But according to Hogan—and Matsuda's wife, for what it's worth—Matsuda put Bollea on the mat, sank his elbow into his shin, and cranked his foot until he heard a crack.

Bollea screamed. He said he thought his ankle was broken and that he had to get to the hospital. "Hey, you said you wanted to be a wrestler," grunted Graham. "This is part of it. Sometimes things like this happen in the ring."

"I'll be back," Bollea said. The old wrestlers laughed. "Yeah, sure, you rock 'n' roller. You won't be back."

The way Hogan told it later, the greatest indignity was having to call his dad, a construction foreman, big-handed and spare with his words, to pick him up because he couldn't work the clutch on his car with the bum ankle. His dad read him the riot act for making a fool of himself. Hogan says he spent ten weeks in a cast. (Brisco puts it at six weeks tops.) He sold his college books, his band equipment, his van. He worked on his conditioning. He either moved into a hotel room or else he was already living in a hotel room and moved back home with his parents—either way, a move of some significant shame. After he healed up, he walked back into the Snake Pit. Matsuda admired his resolve and waved him back into the ring. After fifteen minutes of grappling, Hiro told Graham that Bollea was approved. He set about training him, for real this time. A thousand push-ups, a thousand squats. Matsuda worked him hard, simply telling Bollea and the other trainees to "keep up with me." Push-ups, squats. After four months—four months—of grueling, senseless cardio work, Matsuda showed them their first wrestling move. He taught them to shoot—to fight for real; brutal holds and bullying tricks to win a brawl.

There's video of Bollea in these days, and you can see the wooden frame of what would become Hulk Hogan. He's plainly strong but slimmer, lithe like a real athlete. The long hair, lightened but not bleached to its peak form. The handlebar mustache is there in adolescent form, wispy and brown. Muttonchop sideburns remnant from his bass guitar days. There's a sadness in his eyes, a daze, the look of a person stuck in limbo, pacing in half circles between each toss. If you squint you can see an earnestness in his face that belies his superheroic frame. That's part of the Hogan mindset that persisted, though it would eventually inflate to an unworkable size, along with his muscles.

According to Hogan, it was months into this interminable bootcamp—Gerry Brisco recalls that it was relatively shorter than Hogan remembers it—when Eddie Graham finally appeared and brought Hogan into his office and let him in on the secret.

* * *

In the business, the secret is called kayfabe. The word itself was widely thought to be a carnival-lingo pig-latinization of "be fake," but there's compelling evidence that "keep kayfabe" is actually a bastardization of the long-forgotten British schoolboy slang phrase "keep cavey," which meant "be careful" or "keep a lookout," mongrelized through the western European accent of some of pro wrestling's early promoters.

Kayfabe is the insistence that the put-on or pro wrestling is reality, and moreover it's the grammar of the sport, the tacit agreement that turns a lit warehouse or civic arena into a charged theater of belief. It is not merely the lie everyone knows is a lie but the discipline of maintaining it—the code that once required wrestlers to live out their feuds in diners, airports, and courtrooms, long after the bell rang. But kayfabe is less about deception than about atmosphere: the low fog of menace, honor, grievance, and destiny that makes a body slam reverberate like a moral verdict.

In its classical form, kayfabe was a totalizing worldview. Heroes and villains were not roles but conditions of being. The good guy paid his bar tab with tips, the bad guy stiffed the waitress. Wrestlers bled real blood to authenticate unreal wars. Promoters acted as petty sovereigns, enforcing the code with blacklists and broken careers. To violate kayfabe was not to break character but to tear the fabric that separated wrestling from burlesque. Without it, the whole thing risked becoming pantomime, a gymnastic vaudeville.

What makes kayfabe compelling is that it sits at the intersection of folklore and con artistry. It borrows from carnival barkers, from boxing's fixed fights and wrestling's carnival roots, but it also echoes older rituals: medieval morality plays, saints' lives, public executions. The ring is a consecrated square where virtue and vice are rendered legible through flesh. The audience knows the outcome is arranged, but they also know that pain is not. This double consciousness—belief suspended but not abandoned—is the engine of the form.

Subcultures may invent their own laws to survive in the cracks of official society, and kayfabe belongs squarely in that lineage. It is a parallel reality sustained by shared silence. Like the underworld slang of thieves or the secret routes of flâneurs, kayfabe creates insiders and outsiders. To be "smart" to the business was to possess forbidden knowledge, and yet true sophistication lay in knowing when not to deploy it. The most devoted fans were those who could see the strings and still weep when the puppet died.

The collapse of kayfabe in the late twentieth century—its public disavowal, its conversion into metacommentary—did not kill wrestling, but it changed its texture. Irony replaced sincerity; winks replaced oaths. Wrestlers now speak openly of "the business," yet still ask for belief when the lights go down. Kayfabe survives in fragments, in moments when the crowd forgets itself and roars as if the outcome were not already sealed. It persists because it answers a persistent hunger: the desire for stories that are simple, brutal, and absolute, even if only for an evening.

In the end, kayfabe is not a fraud but a folk art. It is the collective decision to treat a staged conflict as if it mattered, because meaning often requires rehearsal. The ring teaches us how easily conviction can be summoned, how eagerly we collaborate in our own enchantment. And when it works, when the illusion holds, kayfabe reminds us that truth is sometimes less important than intensity, and that belief, even temporary belief, can still land with the force of a real blow.

That's the long version. Some people might just say it's professional wrestling's big lie. When Terry Bollea walked into the Sportatorium the first time, he certainly had an idea that wrestling wasn't on the level. That's why Matsuda was so brutal. They had to beat the disbelief out of everyone and send them back out into the world to preach the gospel. Once they proved they were in it for the long haul, trainees got read into the order. Bollea had finally made it.

He had his first match—a trial by fire—against Hector "Don" Serrano in late 1977. Serrano entered the ring first, and when Bollea walked out next, the arena went silent. Not a disrespectful silence but awe. By the time he got into the ring, the crowd had erupted into a standing ovation, just because of the look of the guy. He wrestled the next night in Fort Myers against Brian Blair, who would go on to be half of the Killer Bees tag team in the WWF. (Unsurprisingly, in Blair's recollection, he was Hogan's first opponent.) They wrestled again a few days later up the road in Chiefland. They were told it would be a fifteen-minute draw, so the two rookies planned out a match. They thought they were doing a good job because they could see all the other wrestlers gathered by the curtain to watch them. When they hit the fifteen-minute mark, exhausted, they heard the ring announcer call out over the microphone, "There are five minutes remaining." Five minutes later, the voice boomed again: "Five minutes remaining." Bollea and Blair realized they were being ribbed—pranked, in the parlance of the locker room. Already exhausted, they had to vamp for the second half of the match while the wrestlers at the curtain laughed. The rib meant that he was one of them, and acceptance was the final stage of the cross. It was in that moment that Bollea became a pro wrestler.

Matsuda had taught him the gospel of pain: that a man's worth in the ring was not in his muscles but in his endurance, his ability to sell agony and resurrection in the same breath. Wrestling is theater, sure, but it is also baptism—every slam a cleansing, every drop of blood a story. The story isn't true, not entirely, because it wouldn't be pro wrestling if it was. What matters is why we tell these stories. Every hero has an origin story, but for Hogan, who would spend much of the rest of his career on top of the industry, it was important to establish that he went through the same hell as anybody else, that he rose from the ashes before he even learned his first hold. And maybe more important than anything, the story wants to tell us that even if professional wrestling isn't straight, it's still brutal. In a fixed sport, wins and losses don't matter. Living through it is the real victory.

CHAPTER 2

THE SEARCHER

HULK HOGAN VS. VERNE GAGNE

According to many, the inception of Hulkamania occurred when Hulk Hogan stomped into the ring at Madison Square Garden and beat the Iron Sheik for the WWF championship on January 23, 1984. The Garden had the air of a boiler room: steam rising from coats, beer, breath, the collective impatience of people who had come to see the fulfillment of their primal urges. They all felt what would happen that night was inevitable, but it was so important, so necessary that tension ran viciously. You could feel the architecture lean inward, the rafters conspiring. This was New York in the early Reagan years—roughened, loud, a city that liked its myths broad and legible.

The Iron Sheik arrived first, odd for the defending champion, the man who had ended Bob Backlund's five-year reign at the top of the company and, in the Northeast at least, the wrestling world. The Sheik—real name Hossein Khosrow Ali Vaziri—was a villain imported whole, an actual Iranian in a world filled with Hawaiian Japanese and Italian Arabs, a sociopolitical signifier and real-life brute; he was an actual Olympic wrestler for his home country who escaped for his own safety and was eventually trained into the American profession by Verne Gagne himself. (The "Iron" in his name was to distinguish him from The [Original] Sheik, aka Ed Farhat, the Lebanese-American army vet who popularized the Sheik archetype and, later, a violent style that would lead to hardcore wrestling. Farhat was a mainstay of the Michigan wrestling scene for decades, but he was a star villain at Madison Square Garden in the '50s and '60s, and Vaziri's Iron Sheik played off that notoriety.)

Traditionally, the champion entered last, but not tonight: Hogan's immediate significance, his undeniable singularity—he had only arrived back at the WWF three weeks prior—made him the main attraction, belt or no. As the Iron Sheik stood alone in the ring, the booing was immediate and visceral, as if the crowd had been rehearsing all week. Then Hogan came out, incandescent, less a man than a sign—bandanna, tan, that improbable physique like a billboard flexed into human form. When the bell rang, the match itself was almost beside the point. The story had already been agreed upon in the aisles and at the hot dog stands.

The decisive moment—Hogan "Hulking up," the leg drop, the referee's hand striking the mat—released a sound that felt geological. People hugged strangers. Grown men wept with the seriousness usually reserved for births and funerals. It was patriotism without policy, triumph without cost. The WWF Championship changed hands, but more important, a new grammar was installed: good and evil simplified, victory assured if you believed hard enough.

The crowd erupted, and a new era of pro wrestling was born. That was, by most accounts, the creation of a hero and a movement and one of the most lucrative eras in pro wrestling history. This is, as most things are in the history of pro wrestling, a distorted truth, a streamlined version to tell a bigger story. We'll get to that story, but first let's backtrack nine months to a different world title match also featuring Hulk Hogan. His opponent wasn't an Iranian menace but rather a bleached-blond Missourian named Nick Bockwinkel, with a mean streak and an exceptional vocabulary. The championship in question was the AWA World Title.

* * *

The American Wrestling Association in the early 1980s was not a logical place for the birth of a secular demigod. In the pro wrestling universe, it was a place of order, of inherited logic, of craftsmanship polished to a dull gleam. Its center of gravity was Minneapolis, not Manhattan; its moral compass pointed toward labor, not hype. The AWA believed in wrestling as a practiced skill, a trade, not a show. And yet it was here that Terry Bollea was given his first extended opportunity to test what would soon metastasize into Hulkamania, that airborne contagion of patriotism, muscle, and staged grievance that would come to dominate American pop culture in the Reagan years.

Hogan's AWA run, from late 1981 through early 1984, has often been dismissed as a prelude, an awkward adolescence before the glossy adulthood of the WWF. This does it a disservice. The AWA was not simply a waiting room; it was a proving ground and a stage all its own. Much is made of Hogan's in-ring technique whenever a video surfaces of his Japanese work around this period, and certainly the expectations of the Japanese form brought out the best in him, but the AWA was a world of similar levels of tradition. It forced Hogan to work within limits—stylistic, ideological, economical—and in doing so revealed, by contrast, exactly what Hulkamania required in order to detonate. If the WWF was the explosion, the AWA was the pressure cooker, the sealed environment where volatile ingredients learned what they were capable of becoming.

The AWA was old America. Verne Gagne, its patriarch, embodied a postwar ideal of sporting masculinity: collegiate credentials, Olympic dreams, the notion that legitimacy flowed from technique and endurance rather than from spectacle alone. In Gagne's universe, champions were craftsmen who happened to draw money, not attractions who happened to wrestle. The AWA audience reflected this worldview. They came to be convinced, not dazzled. They believed they could tell a true wristlock from a sham.

And yet there was Hulk Hogan. (To be fair, there was also Jesse "The Body" Ventura, another "Superstar" Billy Graham disciple who predated Hogan in the AWA. The promotion wasn't all substance over form.) In comparison to Gagne and the current world champion Nick Bockwinkel, Hogan was a walking billboard for excess. Even before Hulkamania was fully articulated, his body was already a provocation. He did not look like a wrestler as the AWA faithful had come to expect them—he looked like a Hollywood actor playing a wrestler, like an abstract idea manifest in hard reality. He was too tall, too wide, too theatrically blond. His muscles were not merely developed; they were exaggerated, almost editorialized. In the AWA locker room, where bodies tended toward the solid and the workmanlike—the kind of place where multiple frames have been compared to beer kegs—Hogan was less built for a barnstorming sport, and more for a role in a drive-in epic. If the AWA's existing specimens, guys like The Crusher and Dick the Bruiser, were impressively blocky, sheer masses of muscled meat, Hogan's physique was unfathomably contoured, like something imported from a different genre.

* * *

It had been a winding road to this point. After his initial training, Hogan wrestled around the Southeast before he quit. The Briscos went and found him working on the docks, a good living in those days, and dragged him back into the business. Terry Funk, maybe the best pro wrestler who ever lived, remembers working with young Bollea. He called up Vincent K. McMahon, the elder Vince, father of the modern-day impresario Vincent J.—and told him he should give "Boulder" a look. (Hogan remembers that it was the Briscos that put him in touch with McMahon, but Funk's recollection is compelling.)

McMahon was the pro wrestling promoter in the Northeast, and New York City, divided into neighborhood enclaves of immigrant groups, liked an ethnic superstar. Track the immigration numbers into Ellis Island and watch the representative pro wrestlers pop up in their wake. The Irish had Danno O'Mahoney, the

Greeks had Jim Londos, the Italians had Bruno Sammartino, the Puerto Ricans had Pedro Morales. By the time Bollea walked in, Vince Sr. needed something new for the Irish crowd. There was Davey O'Hannon, but he never really caught on, not like Dominic DeNucci or Ivan Putski or Chief Jay Strongbow had for their audiences. So Terry Bollea got the role.

Hogan, a good solid Irish name. They took "Hulk" from the name he used in Memphis and around other parts—Terry "The Hulk" Boulder. ("Sterling Golden" was the other name, depending on the promotion.) The story goes that "Terry Boulder" was on a local talk show the same day Lou Ferrigno, the muscle-bound star of *The Incredible Hulk*, was on, and Bollea towered over him, so promoter Jerry Jarrett decided to borrow the nickname. This story is widely accepted as fact, though no one has seen the tape of the show, and Ferrigno doesn't seem to remember it.

Jarrett debuted him in the CWA with a video package featuring Bollea flexing in shadows and a booming movie voice-over by local announcer Michael St. John:

> This man is not a television illusion . . . he is not a figment of the imagination . . . He stands an amazing six foot seven inches tall. He weighs an incredible 324 pounds. He is the Hulk. The Hulk without a doubt is the most awesome figure in professional wrestling today.

Hogan carried that aura with him wherever he went, even if his ring work and mic skills didn't yet back up the mythos. In that first run in the WWWF, he was stiff in the ring and marble-mouthed on the microphone, pasting phrases borrowed from "Superstar"

Billy Graham, Austin Idol, and Dusty Rhodes together with none of their artistry, but all of this was hidden by his look and by virtue of his playing the villain—a sneaky tool used in the wrestling world to simplify the process for newcomers—and by pairing him with loquacious manager "Classy" Freddie Blassie. His most famous match in the WWWF was in Shea Stadium against André the Giant in 1980. The match featured two of the most physically awesome wrestlers in the world, lasted under eight minutes, and yet was despite all of that fairly boring. The highlight was Hogan slamming André—a moment conveniently forgotten by the time the two feuded again in 1987, but one wishes the whole match could be memory-holed. The only real excitement came after the match—first, Hogan seemed to kick out of the pin, but the referee still announced André the winner. This is the kind of cover you would usually see for a heroic underdog—he lost but only due to the transgression of the referee—but here it was the evil Hogan who was inexplicably given the benefit of the doubt. Afterward Hogan slipped a diabolical piece of metal into the sleeve of his elbow pad and clocked André, busting him open, and then abruptly left the ring. It's impossible to see André, the winner by error, bleeding profusely beneath his mythic afro, and understand the decision-making behind it all. It felt more like a beginning than an ending. For Hogan's career, perhaps that's the metaphor.

According to Greg Gagne, son of Verne, who also wrestled on that card, Hogan was so distraught after his poor performance in the match that he considered walking away from the sport yet again, but the younger Gagne convinced him to come up to Minnesota, where they could teach him how to really work.

There's a much more accepted version of Hogan's departure

from the WWWF, which is that Sylvester Stallone reached out to cast him in *Rocky III*, and Vince Sr. flatly refused to let him do it, concerned that a wrestler playing a wrestler in a movie would undermine the legitimacy of the sport. Sure, the argument seems ridiculous on its face, but it wasn't an uncommon one in a time where the top priority was "protecting" the business from insinuations of inauthenticity. But (assuming the story is true) Vince Sr. missed the point—the allure—of Hogan altogether. He was inherently ridiculous. Ridiculous in stature, in affect, and in performance. You couldn't look at a Hogan match and believe it in any traditional way. Hulk Hogan would soon be bigger than the sport itself because—not in spite of the fact that—he was too amazingly ridiculous to be taken seriously, or, more important, to be perceived as one taking himself too seriously. Maybe inadvertently, Hulk Hogan seemed to be in on the joke.

Because the elder McMahon wouldn't let him film *Rocky III*, Hulk left the WWWF. He was working regularly in Japan, so he had some money, and he was determined to make the movie, to expand his stardom, to expand his horizons. He eyed a stardom that was bigger than the ring, bigger than Madison Square Garden, bigger than Shea Stadium. But to get there, he had to leave the WWWF. And the AWA was happy to give him a shot.

* * *

The early Hogan in the AWA was not yet the smiling, flag-waving avatar of children's vitamins and arena-sized optimism. He was volatile, sometimes sullen, occasionally monstrous. He was alternatingly positioned as a heel, a babyface, or something unresolved in between. The promotion itself seemed unsure what to do with him, and this uncertainty was instructive. Hogan's charisma was undeniable, but it was also unruly. He drew attention even when he was not meant to. He bent sightlines toward himself. In a promotion built on balance—on a sort of hard-nosed socialism, the idea that no one man should eclipse the whole—this could be a problem.

And yet the crowds reacted. They reacted in ways that unsettled the existing order. Hogan elicited noise that was not polite or knowing but primal, almost embarrassed. It was the sound of people responding to something they had not yet been taught how to process. Children, in particular, gravitated toward him, sensing in his bigness and theatricality a permission to feel loudly. Adults, especially men who prided themselves on discernment, were perhaps more ambivalent. They could see the artifice, and some resented it. But even resentment was a form of attention.

This tension—between the AWA's ethic of earned legitimacy and Hogan's gravitational pull—became the central drama of his run. It was most evident in the question of the championship. Hogan, judging solely by the metric of crowd response, should have been the AWA champion. He was the biggest draw, the most distinct face, the man who made the building feel different when he entered. And yet the belt remained out of reach. Verne Gagne, ever the guardian of his promotion's values, hesitated. To put the title on Hogan would have been to admit that spectacle trumped craft, that size and charisma could outweigh lineage and technique.

Steadily the blueprint became visible. Hogan started wearing promotional T-shirts and hawking them in the parking lot after shows. In interviews he discovered his affection for the fans, and later his patriotism. In one memorable promo aimed at former

AWA champion Masa Saito, Hogan wore a T-shirt with "American Made" printed on the front. In a voice meekly approximating his later, well-known pep rally growl, he said, "Saito, you're gonna face the red, white, and blue. Red because I'm red-hot about the whole situation, and white because I'm a dirty white boy, and blue because that's the color that you're going to be." He apologized for disappearing on the fans during one of his tours of Japan. "This is the great country of America, and you can always change your mind."

The famous standoffs between Hogan and Gagne—both literal and symbolic—have been mythologized into a morality play about stardom and shortsightedness. The truth is more complex. Gagne was not blind to Hogan's appeal; he was wary of its implications. Hogan represented a future in which wrestling would no longer pretend to be sport at all, but would instead declare itself mythology. The AWA was not ready to make that leap. In retrospect, this hesitation looks like a failure of vision. At the time, it was a defense of an entire worldview.

Hogan's matches in the AWA, especially against old-school opponents like Bockwinkel, functioned as dialectics. Bockwinkel was everything Hogan was not: cerebral, verbally agile, a technician who could make superiority feel inevitable rather than overwhelming. When Hogan faced Bockwinkel, the ring became a laboratory for testing audience allegiance. Did the crowd want to admire excellence, or did they want to participate in triumph? Hogan's style—simpler, more explosive, less interested in nuance—invited participation. His comebacks were designed to be felt collectively. The famous "Hulking up" sequence, where Hogan would signal the last stanza of a match by shaking his head and becoming impervious to his opponent's harm, was already a ritual in the AWA, a call-and-response between performer and crowd.

Even if Gagne saw Hogan's inevitability, it's still safe to say that these rituals were not fully sanctioned by the promotion. And that makes Hogan's popularity that much more impressive. In the WWF, Vince McMahon would later understand that wrestling's power lay precisely in this bypass—that the promoter's job was to orchestrate communion with the crowd, not to enforce realism. In the AWA, Hogan's popularity felt like a disruption.

Outside the ring, Hogan was learning how to be a character rather than merely a wrestler. His interviews in the AWA were raw, sometimes awkward, plainly leaning on his fandom of Superstar Graham (who himself copped liberally from Muhammad Ali, who himself cited Freddie Blassie and 1950s wrestling icon Gorgeous George as his influences), right down to calling people "Brother" and referring to his arms as "pythons." But there was a naive marketing genius at play as well. Hulk spoke in slogans before slogans were expected. He framed conflicts as moral tests. He gestured toward an audience that extended beyond the building, as if he already sensed that wrestling's future lay in its ability to reach the masses and leak into everyday life—into living rooms, onto lunchboxes, and into the imaginations of people who did not consider themselves fans.

The AWA, for all its strengths, could not be that stage. Its resistance to crowning Hogan was not merely stubbornness; it was structural. To fully embrace Hogan would have required the AWA to abandon its self-conception as a wrestling promotion and become something closer to a pop-cultural engine. This was not a compromise that Gagne was prepared to make, not yet anyway.

The event itself, dubbed "Super Sunday," was no WrestleMania, and the St. Paul Civic Center, proud as it was, was no Madison Square Garden, and so the night fell a bit short in the pageantry of destiny that the Iron Sheik match later would have. The arena—low-ceilinged, fluorescent, "civic" in the most unromantic sense—held a crowd that knew wrestling the way factory men know machinery: intimately, and with due reverence.

Bockwinkel was older, verbose, and calculated. He wrestled like an accountant who'd discovered leverage: precise, minimizing risk, a villain whose menace was administrative rather than volcanic. He was respected even as he was loathed. He stood plaintiff in the ring as Hogan entered—again, improbably, the challenger entered last. Hulk entered the arena to "Eye of the Tiger," the theme song unsubtly cribbed from *Rocky III*, just like in his early WWF days. (Bockwinkel had no entrance music, and Hogan actually gets his song played twice, once during the entrance and once during his introduction.) He tore off his T-shirt (front: WE WANT THE BELT; back: NOW OR NEVER) and cupped his ears performatively to the crowd, wagging his finger at Bockwinkel. These are hints at the Hulk Hogan that would come to be known to the masses; this is that Hulk Hogan. The only difference between this night and the peak of the Hulkamania movement is time and location. And because of the long-term storytelling in the AWA feud and the lack of geopolitical elements that simplified the WWF match, compared to the Sheik match, the crowd response here felt so much more earned, more organic, more real.

Hogan, younger then, looked unfinished—big, yes, but still learning how to inhabit his size. The match unfolded at a deliberate pace, punctuated by murmurs rather than roars. When Hogan surged, the building stirred; when Bockwinkel cut him off, it settled back into itself.

The finish, as was the case in so many title matches in those days, was ambiguous, unsatisfying by design. Hogan seemingly won the match, but the result was overturned in the immediate aftermath of the pin due to disqualification: Hogan had inadvertently sent Bockwinkel over the top rope earlier in the match; Bockwinkel had Hogan in a sleeper hold, and as Hogan tried to wrest himself free, the champion tumbled off Hogan and onto the floor. Tossing your opponent over the top rope was illegal, no matter the circumstance, and so Hogan's victory was rescinded. (This type of ending, with the hero winning but having the verdict overturned, would come to be known as a "Dusty Finish," for Dusty Rhodes's constant reliance on the trope during his multiple attempts at the NWA title.)

The audience erupted in frustration. There would be no catharsis, no release. On another night, in another match, the boos would perhaps be not furious so much as weary, the sound of people recognizing the limits of the arrangement between righteousness and the constraints of narrative. But Hogan's loss seemed somehow more dire.

Did Hogan have cause to be upset that Verne refused to give him the belt? It's simultaneously an understandable and inane point of contention. A world title isn't a trophy, not an "employee of the month" plaque. It's a prop in a story, often the culmination of a narrative that, if it's told well, could stretch for months or (in the case of Dusty Rhodes) years. The chase—the babyface comer repeatedly vying for the title, only to be duplicitously repelled by the crosswise heel champ—made for a much more compelling long-term narrative. Which is to say that titles in the AWA were not lost or seized; they were managed. Power stayed where it had always been, behind the curtain, in the fine print. From that point of view, Hogan winning the belt isn't the achievement—to be booked into the feud in the first place is. Losing the match should have been one step in a larger story.

After the decision was reversed, the crowd booing angrily, Hogan went nuts and viciously attacked Bockwinkel and his manager, Bobby "The Brain" Heenan, with the title belt. Trash rained down from the rafters as fans expressed their disapproval. It was a precursor of one of the most memorable days of Hogan's career, when he joined the nWo and turned heel for the first time since his ascent. The trash that day is part of the lore, physical evidence of the degree to which the audience was affected by the story. The same implication should be read here, and the sheer rejection of the result by the audience should be viewed as a triumph. The idea that his losing the match was an error by the office seems like post-rationalization. Hogan's loss that night was one of the most electric moments of his entire career. "This is your belt," Hogan boomed to the crowd when interviewed immediately afterward. "I'm the champion, and this is your belt."

Regardless of Gagne's long-term vision (or lack thereof), Hogan was not the face of the AWA, not yet anyway, and soon he was signed away by Vincent K. McMahon—the son of Vincent J.—the new owner of the WWF (Vince Jr. removed a *W* from the acronym). He was determined to remake the professional wrestling world, which, in large part due to Hogan's popularity, he was able to do. And so Hogan's loss to Bockwinkel becomes a metaphor for Gagne's inability to evolve, and Hogan's loss lingers like a lesson.

But revisiting that night, there's a more instructive piece here, and it's that neither Vince McMahon nor the WWF more broadly "created" Hulkamania. (The name itself was swiped from Austin Idol's "Idolmania.") Hulkamania was alive and well in St. Paul before he signed with the WWF.

The tragedy, if there is one, is not that the AWA lost Hogan but that it lost the future he represented. The promotion would continue, dignified and increasingly anachronistic, while the industry it helped build moved on without it. Hogan, meanwhile, would become less a wrestler than a symbol, less a man than a machine for generating belief. Hulkamania was in its very inception a rebuke to the old guard. The transformation it brought about had its costs—for the medium, for the culture, for Hogan himself—but it also had its origins in the AWA's refusal to grant him everything he wanted.

Hulkamania, when it came, would promise infinity: endless triumph, endless youth, endless applause. The AWA offered finitude. It insisted on limits, on hierarchy, on the idea that even giants must wait their turn. In resisting Hogan, it inadvertently sharpened him. It taught him that success was inextricable from power, but that connection with the crowd could be earned despite what the office wanted. Hulk Hogan mattered in that moment because he exposed the limitations of the old pro wrestling system and, flexing and grimacing, represented everything it could become.

In the end, Hulk Hogan's time in the AWA reads less like a missed opportunity and more like a necessary friction. It was the sound of old America rubbing against the new, of craft resisting spectacle, of realism arguing with myth. From that friction came heat, and from that heat came light, and the explosion that followed was not an accident. And once unleashed, it would change everything, leaving behind only echoes—and the faint smell of smoke in the civic centers where it all began.

CHAPTER 3

THE MEGASTAR

HULK HOGAN VS. CELEBRITY

Hulk Hogan's return to the WWF—or, as modern WWE would probably have you believe, his debut—came on December 28, 1983, on an episode of *Wrestling at the Chase*. The broadcast itself was evidence of the new WWF's dissolution of the previous territory system in pro wrestling. *Wrestling at the Chase* used to be the television home of the St. Louis Wrestling Club, which was at one time the most powerful promotion in the NWA, featuring some of the country's biggest stars, like Harley Race, Gene Kiniski, and Lou Thesz. Its founder and owner, Sam Muchnick, had retired in 1982, and although the St. Louis Wrestling Club soldiered on without him, one of Muchnick's former partners bartered a deal between Vince McMahon, the new owner of the WWF, and the local TV station that owned the name "Wrestling at the Chase" and the time slot.

Local fans who had been watching *The Chase* since 1959 were undoubtedly surprised that Wednesday to see Vince McMahon and Gene Okerlund hosting the show; if they had any concept of the larger pro wrestling scene, they would only know them as the young WWF announcer from the New York territory and the backstage interviewer from the AWA in Minnesota, but most of the audience was probably just wondering where Larry Matysik was. And undoubtedly knowing they had a new audience to win over, McMahon had stacked the card: There was Big John Studd, tag team champs Tony Atlas and Rocky Johnson, "Dr. D" David Shults, Adrian Adonis and Dick Murdoch, and a newcomer to the promotion named Hulk Hogan.

Hogan put the screws to a local nobody named Bill Dixon for about three minutes before he dropped his big leg across him and ended the match. The crowd responded accordingly: It wasn't the rapture of the end of his AWA tenure, but a "Hulk! Hulk! Hulk!" chant did arise spontaneously. "The Incredible Hulk Hogan" is what Okerlund called him repeatedly, presumably until the lawyers from Marvel Comics tracked the WWF down and they dropped "Incredible" by the wayside. (This isn't a joke: Starting in 1984, the WWF and Marvel struck a licensing deal that allowed McMahon and Co. to use "Hulk" for $100 a match and a 1 percent share of merchandise sales. He also couldn't wear green and purple, for the sake of clarity.) Hogan entered the ring to "Eye of the Tiger," as he would until they found a functional replacement; going national certainly had unforeseen consequences in the IP department. There was also a concentrated effort to introduce Hogan to the new audience—both in St. Louis and in the wider WWF world. Okerlund approached the role with the gushing elation of a *Tiger Beat* writer—"He has a number of different hobbies, and actually lives and breathes this great sport of professional wrestling"—while McMahon focused on the visuals: "Look at the way the Hulk is put together. That is all muscle, a mountain of it as well, Gene."

His big return in New York came as a surprise cornerman for WWF champion Bob Backlund. Backlund was supposed to have a match with one of the Wild Samoans, but the other two (and their manager, Lou Albano) kept interfering, so Backlund stomped backstage and returned with Hogan at his hip. The crowd erupted, as if they were prepared for the moment. Perhaps they just looked at Hogan next to the relatively dull, pale body of Backlund and felt compelled to celebrate the distinction. Or perhaps they were as mesmerized by his physique as McMahon clearly was on play-by-play. "That's 300 pounds of aaallllll muscle in there!" he intoned. The reintroduction of Hulk Hogan was moving along according to plan.

The last time these fans had seen Hogan he was a heel. A villain. A dastardly foil set opposite André the Giant, perhaps the most beloved (and feared) wrestler of all time. He wore a cape and was led around by "Classy" Freddie Blassie, one of the Holy Trinity of heel managers in the old WWWF. Blassie was a former wrestler, a bleached-blond, Hollywood-born tough who was notorious for his magnetic promos and for biting his opponents in the forehead until they bled. (In 1983 he released an album entitled "I Bite the Songs.") In his dotage he had retired to the managerial life, wearing matching short-sleeve-button-down-shirt-and-slacks combos and carrying around a cane that was employed liberally as a weapon. He was known for representing the Iron Sheik, Killer Khan, and (briefly, for his match against legendary wrestler Antonio Inoki in Japan) Muhammad Ali. With Blassie by his side Hogan couldn't help but get booed. But now, on his own, the crowd couldn't help but cheer him.

He had Backlund's blessing, too. Interviewed after the match, Backlund said, "Everybody knows the Hulk. He's changed his ways. He's a great man. He's told me he's not going to have Blassie around." At which point Hogan commandeered the mic, thanked the WWF for bringing him back, and tore off his shirt. In a few short words, Backlund had ceded not just the microphone but the spotlight to Hogan. The crowd screamed at his first words, seemingly excited to have something to be excited about. Hulk Hogan was different from what preceded him in the WWF—Bruno Sammartino had been megapopular, sure, but one only needed to look at Hogan standing next to Backlund to visualize the evolution of the sport. Moreover, he was modern and uniquely relevant, a reflection of the sudden shift in the culture at large. Pro wrestling is at its best when it reflects the world around it; Hogan carried a gigantic metaphorical mirror in on his mountainously muscled back.

* * *

On January 23, 1984, in Madison Square Garden, Hulk Hogan took on the Iron Sheik for the WWF title. It was not merely a wrestling match; it was a handoff, a change in management of the national dream. When Hulk Hogan pinned the Iron Sheik and took the

World Wrestling Federation championship, it felt like a landslide election—an inauguration disguised as a leg drop.

Professional wrestling has always trafficked in metaphors too large to be believable and therefore irresistible. Its business is exaggeration; its product is certainty. In a decade increasingly uncertain about itself—economically, politically, morally—wrestling offered something bracingly simple: good guys and bad guys, right flags and wrong flags, heroes who flexed and villains who sneered. On that January night, the WWF crowned a new champion, and in doing so it selected a mascot for the 1980s, a living billboard for excess, confidence, and the idea that problems could be solved by getting bigger than them.

The Iron Sheik entered the ring draped in hostility. Born Hossein Khosrow Ali Vaziri in Iran, he had been repurposed into a geopolitical shorthand: the boastful foreigner, the enemy made flesh. His presence carried with it the stale smoke of nightly news broadcasts and the echo of embassy crises. He was not supposed to be liked; he existed to be extinguished. His championship reign—brief, tense, almost administrative—functioned as a holding pattern while the company prepared its transition from Backlund to Hogan. Sheik was a segue between the two men, a villainous semicolon.

(The Iron Sheik was farcical, too; so were the Samoans. The foreign heels often were. They leaned into the stereotypes to paint in the broadest strokes possible. In a world filled with "regular" guys, they stood out and scandalized the crowd. As the WWF would soon prove, when such farces made up the entire roster, the product was moving into the broadest territory possible, a place where cliché meant simplicity meant ease of communication meant power.

With Hogan at the helm, wrestling was about to announce itself as spectacle rather than sport.)

The Iron Sheik was never meant to be a long-term antagonist. He was a narrative device. A heat generator. A symbolic transfer station. Iran, in the American imagination, had been flattened into menace. Wrestling didn't invent that—it exploited it. Hogan defeating the Iron Sheik in January 1984 introduced this new protagonist as the embodiment of American triumph. That match was not great, but it was undeniably *legible*. The story required no context. You could drop into it cold and understand everything. This was Vince's genius, too. He wasn't chasing realism. He was chasing clarity.

Hulk Hogan, by contrast, arrived already inflated with promise. He was a slogan with arms. Hogan's look was all primary colors and loud geometry: yellow, red, blond, tan. (He appeared sunburned by destiny.) When he flexed, he was aiming at the camera, not the crowd, as though the future had already been storyboarded and he was simply hitting his marks.

Madison Square Garden, that venerable civic interior, has hosted everything from political conventions to ice shows, but wrestling nights transformed it into something closer to a cathedral of noise. The crowd doesn't sit; it perches, leans, vibrates. It participates. Pro wrestling has never been passive entertainment. It is ritualized shouting, communal judgment rendered through volume; without the crowd's reaction pro wrestling loses all meaning. On this night, the boos that followed the Sheik felt like an obligation, while the cheers for Hogan came preloaded, like a chorus waiting for its cue.

The match itself was almost beside the point. It was efficient, symbolic, clean. Hogan broke the Sheik's hold, rose as if from the dead, flexed, struck, dropped the leg. The referee counted. The building detonated. There was little suspense, but sometimes the best wrestling experience is an expected outcome that makes you feel for just a moment like it's happening for the first time. The crowd cheered, though they were certainly not surprised.

If wrestling were only about athletic competition, this moment would not still matter. But wrestling is about narrative authority—who gets to embody the story a culture wants to tell itself. In the early 1980s, America was eager for a reset. The hangover from the previous decade lingered: inflation, cynicism, the residue of loss. The rhetoric of the era promised restoration through strength, optimism through volume. Hulk Hogan fit this promise perfectly. He was not subtle enough to lie.

The Iron Sheik, meanwhile, was cast as a problem that strength could solve. His villainy was not personal so much as symbolic. He represented the outside world's refusal to conform to the vague standards of modernity, and wrestling solved that refusal the only way it knows how: by pinning it flat on its back for three seconds. The ethics of this spectacle are worth examining, but wrestling has never claimed moral complexity. It trades in emotional clarity, and clarity requires contrast.

What happened that night was also a business maneuver executed with theatrical precision. The WWF was in the midst of its transformation from a regional promotion into a national brand. Hulk Hogan was scalable in a way few wrestlers had ever been. His appeal translated instantly into posters, lunchboxes, cartoon appearances. He did not require explanation. He was a logo that talked.

❁ ❁ ❁

By 1983, the tide had turned. The world was different now—louder, shinier, hungry for spectacle. The American concept of body was changing, too: movie stars with chiseled physiques, gyms on every corner, Ronald Reagan on the television preaching strength and morning in America. It was the perfect climate for a hero, though not the kind who read books or wore suits. (I mean this broadly, though it's worth noting that, upon his return to the WWF years later in 1992 as a heel, Backlund's character did both.) The old mythology had grown stale, and the people wanted a new version, a, well, more muscular version—something that could look them in the eye and promise, without irony, that good would triumph if you just believed hard enough.

Terry Bollea, by then fully metamorphosed into Hulk Hogan, walked straight into the void America had carved for him. A visionary in the language of excess, McMahon saw what others had missed: that wrestling could be not just sport but scripture. He signed Hogan and rebranded the World Wrestling Federation as a kind of electric church. The ring became a pulpit; the promo, a sermon.

And Hogan preached. He preached not just with his words but with his arms, with his chest, with that strange, growling baritone that filled stadiums like thunder. Train, say your prayers, eat your vitamins—a gospel as American as cornflakes, as self-invented as the suburbs. The crowds came in waves, and when the kids started lining up in numbers, McMahon knew they were on to something. They chanted Hogan's name as if it were an incantation, as if the syllables themselves could make him stronger.

It wasn't subtle, but it was sincere. Hogan's every gesture was outsize, almost innocent in its grandeur. When he ripped his shirt open, it was a ritual shedding of doubt; when he pointed to the crowd, he made them complicit in his myth. Hogan was at once otherworldly and relatable; the boundaries between fan and performer, fiction and faith dissolved under the klieg lights. Children mean-mugged at their reflections in the mirror, mimicking his monologues. Hulkamania wasn't just a craze; it was a kind of populist mysticism, a belief that inside every ordinary person was a larger, louder self waiting to break free.

By the time he pinned the Iron Sheik in Madison Square Garden, taking the WWF title and setting off a nationwide tremor of cheers, it was prophecy fulfilled. The boy from Tampa had been rewritten by America itself, reconstituted as an emblem of triumph. In that moment, Hulk Hogan stopped being a man entirely. He became an idea—a motion, a sound, an idea of invincibility.

* * *

When Hulk Hogan returned to the World Wrestling Federation in December 1983, almost nobody—not the wrestlers, not the promoters, not even the fans—understood what that return actually meant. It was more than just a second chance, and more than a reset. No, this time was different, and not in a way that was immediately visible. The difference was not Hogan's size, which had always been absurd. It wasn't his charisma, which had always been obvious, even when it was clumsy. It wasn't even his growing celebrity, though *Rocky III* mattered more than wrestling people were comfortable admitting. The difference was the company he was returning to—and, more specifically, the man running it.

Vince McMahon was no longer the son running his father's territory. He was a would-be monopolist. He didn't want to win wrestling. He wanted to *end* it, at least as it had existed. The return of Hulk Hogan was not a nostalgic move. It was a new beginning—a business model being activated.

Before Hulk Hogan could jump-start the 1980s wrestling boom, he had to destroy the territorial system: a loose, paranoid, gentleman's-agreement network of regional promotions that had defined professional wrestling for decades. Territories were conservative by design. They had to be. Each one depended on predictability: predictable champions, predictable cycles, predictable audiences. Television was local. Touring was regional. Growth was incremental. The business wasn't about expansion; it was about maintenance. Stars mattered, but only within limits. If someone got too popular, they either bought into an ownership stake or they left for greener pastures. If they became too famous, they might disrupt the ecosystem. Wrestling, for most of its history, was built to keep everyone at the same altitude.

The World Wide Wrestling Federation was perhaps the most powerful territory of them all, anchored by Madison Square Garden and the Northeast Corridor. But even it operated under the same unwritten rules. Champions came and went. Promoters protected their borders. Nobody was supposed to think bigger than the map. Vince McMahon Jr. did. Cable television invalidated the whole system. Suddenly, geography was optional. Wrestling could be anywhere, everywhere, all at once. Most promoters responded by tightening their grip on what they already had. Vince responded by expanding in every direction.

It's tempting—especially in hindsight—to frame Hulk Hogan as Vince McMahon's *plan*. He wasn't. He was the tool. The plan was national syndication, centralized branding, and vertical integration before wrestling had language for any of those things. Vince didn't want to be first among equals. He wanted to be the only game in town. To do that, he had to break three rules at once: (1) Pay for television time instead of selling it; (2) Poach talent from other territories openly; and (3) Create stars bigger than wrestling itself.

The first rule was the most dangerous. For most promotions, the TV show was functionally a commercial to get people to the live shows, but actively paying for TV was a bet that content itself—not local loyalty—would drive revenue. It meant front-loading risk in exchange for long-term control. This was not how wrestling people thought. This was how media companies thought. The second rule made Vince enemies everywhere. Wrestling had survived on trust, such as it was. Handshake agreements. Vince replaced trust with leverage. The third rule is where Hulk Hogan enters the story—not as destiny but as solution.

Hulk Hogan was entirely self-evident. He was tall, blond, tan, and built like a monument to gym membership. You didn't need to understand wrist locks or finishes to understand what Hulk Hogan was supposed to be. He looked like the answer to a question America was already asking itself in the early 1980s: What if strength were simple again?

Rocky III—which Vince's father didn't want Hogan to do—was, ironically, the linchpin. It didn't just make Hogan famous—it made him comprehensible to nonwrestling audiences. The *Rocky* movies themselves were legendary works of sports mythology with an audience that outstripped that of pro wrestling. Coopting that audience was key for pro wrestling's expansion into the mainstream. That boxing and wrestling resemble each other from a distance mattered less than the more implicit connection: Rocky and wrestling were both morality plays told through staged sports. Thunderlips, his character in the film, wasn't subtle, but subtlety wasn't the goal. The point was that Hogan could be placed in a mainstream narrative and still feel like he belonged there. Vince didn't just want a wrestler who could draw wrestling fans. He wanted someone who could recruit new ones.

The Rock 'n' Wrestling Connection—Hogan and the WWF's crossover into the pop music universe—which followed Hogan's championship win, is often remembered as kitsch: Cyndi Lauper, MTV, pop excess. It *was* that, but it was also infrastructure. Vince didn't just want wrestling fans watching MTV. He wanted MTV fans watching wrestling. Cross-promotion was customer acquisition. Hogan was the hinge because he didn't need wrestling for him to make sense. He could appear anywhere and remain Hulk Hogan. The same could not be said for most wrestlers.

By the early 1980s, professional wrestling was already an exercise in controlled nostalgia. But even in the arena of nostalgia, its rituals started to feel old. The business had always depended on bodies that could signify something instantly, but cable television had accelerated the need for legibility. Faces had to read from a distance; motives had to fit inside a promo; heroes had to make sense without explanation.

He had passed through other worlds first: Florida, Japan, the AWA, the movies. Each left a mark. In Florida he learned the trade.

In the AWA he learned the craft—and learned how to be a star. In Japan he learned scale—how to be large without rushing, how to let a crowd absorb you before you moved. In Hollywood he learned that size alone was not enough; you had to hold the frame. His brief appearance in *Rocky III* was a test of whether his presence could survive outside wrestling's protected ecosystem. Whether he could be undeniable.

McMahon often talks about how he wanted to bring wrestling out of the smoke-filled armories and bingo halls it had inhabited when he took over. (His father had run monthly shows at Madison Square Garden, but the point stands.) But Vince was not so much interested in making wrestling respectable; he was interested in making it unavoidable. The WWF in 1983 was at a moment in which it would decide what it was going to become. It was shedding its provincial skin, repositioning itself as a national—and eventually global—entertainment machine. Hogan's recruitment was not incidental to this shift. It was foundational. You do not expand without a symbol.

Hogan's values—competition, loyalty, self-belief framed as morality—were compatible with the WWF's expansionist logic. He could be positioned as both champion and ambassador. He made wrestling safe for advertisers without making it small. He reassured parents while thrilling children. This dual appeal is rare and valuable, and Vince McMahon moved quickly to secure it. Traits that did not serve the central narrative were discarded. Irony, vulnerability, introspection—these were unnecessary. What remained was volume. Wrestling became louder because Hogan functioned best with the knob cranked up all the way.

There is a tendency, in hindsight, to treat Hogan's rise as inevitable. This is a mistake. Wrestling history is littered with bodies that looked promising but failed to resonate. Hogan's success required timing, infrastructure, and a willingness by the promotion to commit fully to his elevation. The recruitment of Hogan was also a gamble by McMahon—a bet that the audience would follow a single figure wherever he led. That bet reshaped the business. Once Hogan was positioned as the future, everything else bent accordingly. Storylines simplified. Villains were calibrated for contrast rather than complexity. The audience was trained to read matches as moral showdowns rather than athletic contests. Hogan's recruitment represents the adoption of a new philosophy.

Television was the silent partner in this recruitment. Cable expanded the available audience; syndication multiplied exposure. Hogan was camera ready in a way that earlier wrestling stars had not needed to be. He understood how to pause for reaction, how to let a gesture land. His body language was instructional. Watch me. Believe this. React now.

The WWF's decision to build around Hogan also reflected a shift in how wrestling understood authenticity. In earlier eras, authenticity had meant believability—could this man really fight? By 1983, authenticity had been redefined as consistency. Could this character be trusted to behave the same way everywhere, every time? Hogan passed this test easily. He was predictable, and predictability became a virtue.

Where once the objective was to find the best wrestler, McMahon was looking for an avatar. Hogan did not need to be the most technically skilled. He needed to be durable, legible, and willing to subsume himself into the company's narrative. He needed to be comfortable becoming larger than himself. This comfort would later become a liability, but in 1983 it was an asset. Wrestling was preparing to scale, and scaling requires simplification. Hogan simplified everything he touched. Matches shortened. Stakes clarified. Outcomes felt preordained but also satisfying. The audience learned to want what it was given.

Yet the story is not purely transactional. Hogan believed in the persona as much as the company did. His sincerity, however performative, mattered. Audiences sense contempt quickly. Hogan never appeared embarrassed by wrestling's excesses. He embraced them. The WWF didn't fully come out of the closet as being a staged sport until 1989, but the audiences knew. Part of the specific magic of pro wrestling is that during the show, wrestlers and fans all interact as if it's real, but even the fans of 1983 knew it was not. It holds up as long as wrestling holds our attention, and in 1983 attention was beginning to waver. Then came Hogan, a living god with a spotlight instead of a halo, and the crowds were back in. His inherent excess—his ridiculousness—actually served to enhance the experience. He was so over the top that he solved the eternal question about wrestling's reality. His lack of embarrassment functioned as a permission structure. Viewers could cheer without irony.

Before Hogan, pro wrestling was a patchwork. After him, it was a brand. This transformation carried costs—flattened narratives, reduced diversity of style—but it also ensured survival. Wrestling adapted to a new media environment by choosing a figure that could bear the weight of visibility. In 1983, it was not yet obvious that the WWF would claim the national imagination. Hogan was simply another returning star, albeit a conspicuously large, tanned one. But Hogan's arrival was not about the present moment. It was about anticipation. The WWF saw in Hogan not just a champion but a future tense.

* * *

The 1980s were not subtle, politically or culturally. It was an era of restoration fantasies: strength regained, pride reclaimed, order reasserted. Ronald Reagan sold America a story about itself. Hulk Hogan was Reaganism without policy. He believed in self-reliance, hard work, clean living, and winning decisively. He didn't question systems. He conquered obstacles. He didn't need irony. He needed enemies.

The Iron Sheik would be the first of many. His loss to Hogan retains its charge because it is so naked in its intention. After the match, Hogan stood in the ring with the belt held high, already sweating into legend. His grin suggested not joy but relief, as though the weight he had been carrying had finally been transferred into gold.

The belt itself mattered. As Hogan learned in the AWA, wrestling championships are not won, they are assigned; but the audience consents to the assignment through belief. On that night, belief came easily. The crowd did not question whether Hogan deserved the title. He looked like the future, and the future had a way of making room for itself.

In the years that followed, this match would be replayed, referenced, mythologized. It would become a cornerstone in the WWF's self-narration, the opening chapter in a story about expansion, spectacle, and dominance. WrestleMania would soon follow, then the explosion of pop-cultural crossovers. Hogan would become both omnipresent and, eventually, exhausting. But on that night, exhaustion had not yet set in. The promise was still fresh, the volume still thrilling.

Looking back, it is tempting to read irony into the scene, to see the seeds of excess and collapse already sprouting. But history rarely announces its regrets in advance. At the moment of Hogan's victory, what prevailed was a sense of arrival. Something had landed. The crowd left that night humming with the certainty that they had witnessed a beginning.

Wrestling, like any durable popular art, survives by adapting its myths to the moment. On January 23, 1984, it adapted perfectly. It offered a hero who could carry the decade on his shoulders. Hulk Hogan mattered in that moment and in the decade that followed because he was the living representation of everything we as a culture were striving for and dreaming of. We couldn't all be Hulk Hogan, but we could say our prayers and take our vitamins and dream. Hogan stepped forward into a role nobody realized needed filling, chest out, arms raised, already larger than the ring that contained him.

The future, it turned out, was blond, loud, and very sure of itself.

CHAPTER 4

THE GIANT KILLER

HULK HOGAN VS. ANDRÉ THE GIANT

On March 29, 1987, professional wrestling staged a magic trick so audacious that it still feels incredible four decades later. WrestleMania III featured Hulk Hogan versus André the Giant; a testament to the notion that the impossible could happen. In a building better known for football and monster trucks than for mythology, 93,000 people—or something like that; wrestling has always preferred a good story to a precise number—sat in the Pontiac Silverdome and agreed, for one afternoon, to believe. The match itself ran less than thirteen minutes and featured fewer moves than a match a third its length, but its genius was in how it made the weight of the past press down on the present, how it sold gravity as an adversary, and how it turned a simple act—one man lifting another—into a referendum on the limits of the human body and the possibility of American spectacle.

The Hogan-André match is often remembered as a triptych of photographs: First, Hogan and André facing off at the beginning of the match, a tremble seemingly evident in Hogan's broad shoulders, and André staring glassily down upon Hogan, considering him like a deity passing judgment on a mortal. Second, André with his arms wrapped around Hogan's waist in a bear hug, squeezing—or attempting to squeeze—the life out of Hogan's body, while Hogan reaches out his arms hopelessly and grimaces, terrified. Third, Hogan hoisting André into the air for a body slam, the pain of the effort writ broadly on Hogan's face, André suspended in the air like the collapsing statue of a deposed despot.

Professional wrestling is a sport that exists only in motion, but that last image could have been the logo for an era, the visual shorthand for wrestling's leap from regional oddity to global carnival. But the photograph lies, or at least simplifies. The drama built into the match was about whether Hogan could win, and furthermore if he could slam André. But more significantly, it was about whether wrestling could convince us that this was the first time it had ever been possible.

To understand why that question mattered, you have to understand André's otherworldly body, his structure, as a narrative. Long before WrestleMania III, André was already a walking epilogue, a living coda to the freak-show tradition that wrestling both inherited and sanitized. His size was not merely large; it was story-sized. Every inch of André's seven-foot, four-inch frame served as an affront to expectations, a reminder that nature sometimes refuses to play by the rules. For years, wrestling promoters had protected his inevitability by insisting that André was undefeated, invincible, a spectacle beyond competition. He was the mountain that could move, the attraction that did not lose or disappoint. Even when André did fail to win, which he did, the losses were treated like clerical errors or local customs, politely ignored by the larger mythology.

Hogan, by contrast, was not inevitable—at least not yet, not in narrative terms, anyway. At the start of 1989, he was aspirational. He was the gym mirror come to life, the embodiment of an idea that if you took your vitamins, said your prayers, and believed hard enough, you could bend reality to your will. Hogan was a billboard for effort: tan, symmetrical, cartoonishly muscular, as if the human form had been designed by committee and focus-grouped to within an inch of its life. Where André's size suggested fate, Hogan's muscles suggested choice. That distinction mattered, because WrestleMania III was, at heart, a story about choice confronting fate.

There was a more straightforward objective to the story, though. Wrestling had spent years telling us André could not be body-slammed. Hogan himself had tried, unsuccessfully, in a grainy clip from the late 1970s that the promotion suddenly rediscovered like a long-lost scroll. The clip became evidence, proof that Hogan had once tested the limits and failed. It also became a promise: What failed once might succeed now, under the right lights, in front of the right crowd. The match was framed as a test of physics as much as a contest of skill. The rules were secondary; gravity was the real heel.

In my book *The Squared Circle*, I wrote of this match,

When Hulk Hogan and Andre the Giant met in what is still considered the biggest wrestling match of all time, exaggeration was in the air. According to various contemporary reports, there were 95,000 people on hand at WrestleMania III to see the 7-foot-5, 525-pound Andre square off against the goldenboy Hulk Hogan, who stood 6-foot-8 and weighed 320 pounds and whose biceps measured 24 inches around. Probably the only number in that last sentence that's unimpeachable is the III.

It's simple to say that the idea of truth in the world of pro wrestling is laughable on its face, but it's telling that even the statistics had to be fudged here. Or, perhaps, it's the reverse—that the story was so fantastical that honest facts could not contain it. The oft-told behind-the-scenes story here is almost as good as the on-screen one, and it has, unsurprisingly, shifted with time and depending on the teller. The basic gist is this: André, who had been a special-attraction fan favorite throughout his career, and who had broken down physically, nearly to the point of retirement, was convinced by Vince McMahon to play the bad guy in what would presumably be his last high-profile storyline. (According to Heenan, it was André's idea.) In WWE's retelling, at least, it was a bold move by McMahon and a brave acquiescence by André, because if fans rejected the transformation, André would lose his reputation and the WWF would lose all the money that reputation would have earned. But the ploy worked beautifully, largely thanks to André's impenetrable, stone-faced presence during the lead-up to the match. He looked brainwashed, as overcome by the new boos he was hearing as by his grievance with Hogan. It helped, certainly, that we had been trained to view monsters as villains; André had been so amazing that he had previously defied this stock characterization. Hulk, for his part, was physically overmatched for the first time in his career. Wrestling fans like their heroes to be supermen or underdogs, and for the first and only time in his career, Hogan was both archetypes at once.

If you want to nitpick with actual reality, it should be noted that André the Giant was not actually undefeated over the preceding fifteen years. He had indeed been body-slammed—numerous times—and not least of all by a young wrestler named Hulk Hogan at the Showdown at Shea in 1980. But that was the WWWF, Vince Sr.'s promotion, and as far as Vince McMahon was concerned, reality began with the advent of cable television.

There's a second layer of unreality to parse here, and it's Hogan's own retelling of the match in the following years. According to him, he was unsure whether André was going to actually let him win until the match was over—or, at least, until André called for the body slam spot.

André has long been the subject of wild fantasy even in the locker rooms and in the bleachers, among fans and wrestlers alike. Ric Flair once told me that as a young wrestler, he was told that André had multiple rows of teeth like a shark, and any time he got the opportunity he craned his neck to try and see into his mouth. A being like André invited such fantasy.

In the ring, there were stories about André abusing opponents he didn't like and generally dominating the ring depending on his mood. Even the retelling of "real" stories about André lean heavily on the iconography of the capricious gods of ancient myth. The Hogan-Andre backstage origin story goes that André didn't like Hogan until Hogan presented him with a case of wine on a bus ride they shared on a tour of Japan. (André rode lying down in the back of the bus, where seats had been removed to accommodate him.) By the time they arrived they were both inebriated and finally friendly. But this is another story from Hogan, another tale of him paying his dues—as well as a wink toward mortals making sacrifices to the gods in centuries past. But even as a human, André legitimately had the physical power and the backstage sway to prevent losing any match he didn't want to.

It's true that Hogan couldn't lift André without André allowing him to, and André had notoriously idiosyncratic motivations. And André may be the only wrestler in history whose losses were faker than his wins. If they got into the ring and André decided to rewrite the script and make himself the victor, there was little anyone, even Hogan, could do to stop him. Every great lie has a kernel of truth, after all. But the notion of him deciding to change the ending to the match at the last moment beggars belief.

In Hogan's retelling, though, nobody would tell him how the match was going to end—not André, not Vince, not anyone—so Hulk was left to wait and hope for the best. It's almost as if, in the post-kayfabe reality, Hogan needed the validation of some other reality to consecrate his effort: The match might not have been on the level, the body slam might have been scripted, but the battle was real. What he didn't understand is that reality doesn't make the story any less compelling. The slam doesn't matter because it was real; the slam only matters for what it meant.

❋ ❋ ❋

André's turn against Hogan was portrayed as a betrayal of friendship, but it was really a betrayal of time. André had been one of Hogan's running buddies on Hogan's Saturday-morning cartoon show, *Hulk Hogan's Rock 'n' Wrestling*, so the youngest of fans felt the sting as much as their parents who had watched André in his prime. But now he was older, slower, visibly in pain. His body, once an instrument of awe, had become a ledger of debts. He needed the match as much as the match needed him. Hogan needed it, too, though for different reasons. The 1980s wrestling boom had made him a household name, but it had also made him a symbol, and symbols demand renewal. Hogan had beaten everyone. To stay special, he needed something that could not be reduced to another notch on the belt. He needed to lift the unliftable.

The entire premise of Hulkamania rode on conquering the odds, and so the central struggle of Hulkamania would be constantly resetting the odds in a convincing fashion to give Hogan something compelling to overcome. There's a case that this is the entirety of pro wrestling in a nutshell, a constant cycle of opening Pandora's Box and wrenching it closed again without anyone noticing. But Hogan presented particular problems, due to his size, his longevity, and his media presence; to kids of my generation, it seemed impossible (or unthinkable) that he could ever not win, so building actual suspense was a herculean effort.

WrestleMania 1 saw Hogan and Mr. T facing off against "Rowdy" Roddy Piper and Paul Orndorff, a chapter in the Hogan-Piper rivalry that existed more on cartoons and on lunchboxes than in the ring. Piper was a loudmouthed, weaselly heel, but not an existential threat to Hogan so much as a counterweight to him. (He was the rival squad leader on the cartoon show.) By WrestleMania 2, Vince McMahon started to visualize the future, putting Hogan inside a steel cage against King Kong Bundy, a terrifying fist-shaped brute. I watched Hogan win that match, ribs taped ostentatiously to convince us of his mortality, at a closed circuit showing of the event. When Hogan won that battle, the mythology was codified; it was hard to imagine a bigger, meaner monster in a more terrifying dungeon than that one. Into that void stepped André the Giant.

The transformative moments of the feud occurred not in the ring but on two episodes of *Piper's Pit*, the talk show hosted by Roddy Piper, who had, in the interregnum between the first Wrestlemania and this one, transformed into a fan favorite himself. In the first episode, an impromptu award ceremony saw André receiving a trophy for his (fictitious) fifteen-year undefeated streak, and Hogan receiving a (bigger) trophy for his three-year reign as WWF champ. Ever the egocentric, Hogan was far from magnanimous in his acceptance speech and looked stunned when André then walked out on the ceremony. When André appeared on *Piper's Pit* the following week, it was with his new manager, the despicable Bobby "The Brain" Heenan.

It was a cataclysmic moment, the sound of the very concept of friendship snapping in two. Hogan entered the stage smiling, still playing the loyal champion, still assuming that whatever tension existed could be smoothed over with charisma and backslapping. André stood beside him like a silent verdict, massive and immovable, his face unreadable in that way that made every pause feel intentional.

Piper, acting as both instigator and Greek chorus, kept needling André about his allegiance, about Hogan's spotlight, about who was really using whom. Hogan laughed it off, talked louder, clapped André on the shoulder—the familiar physical shorthand of dominance disguised as affection. And then André moved. No windup, no theatrical flourish. He reached out and grabbed Hogan's crucifix necklace and T-shirt in one enormous fist and pulled. The fabric of the yellow Hulkamania tank top ripped open like paper, the fabric of space-time rending right along with it. The cross accidentally dug into his skin and left a trail of blood—a normal sight for so much of pro wrestling but so rare for the family-friendly WWF product. Hogan's chest was suddenly exposed as a symbol of vulnerability rather than strength. The crowd gasped in a way they wouldn't have for the most destructive power slam. This was more than a wrestling move—it was an act of sacrilegious contempt.

Hogan's shock sold the whole thing. He didn't Hulk up; he froze. His eyes went wide, his mouth open, caught between anger and disbelief, like someone realizing too late that the argument is over. An unscripted trickle of blood ran down Hogan's chest from the crucifix, reality intruding on the proceedings in a blur of passion, and a nod toward the intractable power of the Giant. André didn't roar or posture. He just stood there, holding the torn shirt, having made his point with brutal economy. In that instant, the WrestleMania III build gained all of its meaning. The giant hadn't attacked Hogan's body; he'd attacked the idea that Hogan was untouchable. And once that illusion was ripped open on television, there was no sewing it back together.

❋ ❋ ❋

Inside the Silverdome, the enormous crowd boos André's entrance in such indignant unison that it sounds like static. André and Heenan enter standing in a parade float that looks like a miniature wrestling ring. They use them for most of the entrances that night, but they were created specifically for André—he is too worn down to even make the long walk from the back into the ring. Hogan eschews the cart; he marches into the ring under his own power to the strains of "Real American," his official theme song that had replaced "Eye of the Tiger." ("Real American" was written by Rick Derringer, known for "Rock and Roll Hoochie Koo," for the WWF's 1985 *The Wrestling Album*. It had actually been written for the tag team The U.S. Express, but the team left the company and Hogan took possession of the song—and the sentiment—in December of that year.) This is the most iconic Hogan entrance ever. Whereas a normal person would seem smaller in an arena that size, Hogan somehow grows to fill it. Even in a venue that huge, he has charisma and energy to spare.

The match itself unfolds like a story that knows its ending but refuses to rush there. André dominates early, leaning on Hogan, chopping him, using his mass as a weapon. Hogan sells the weight, collapsing under it, making each step look like an argument with his own legs. This is important, because selling is the art of making the audience complicit. Hogan's pain gives the crowd permission to worry, and worry is the currency of drama. If Hogan looks invulnerable, the slam means nothing. If he looks breakable, the slam becomes a miracle.

When Hogan finally begins to rally, the crowd noise shifts from roar to chant, from awe to encouragement. This is the moment wrestling does what it does best: It turns spectators into participants without ever breaking the fourth wall. The chant is not for Hogan to win; it is for Hogan to *try*. The crowd wants to see the attempt, the honest confrontation with gravity. This is a moral struggle, and victory is almost beside the point.

The slam comes almost out of nowhere. André charges, Hogan sidesteps, and suddenly the giant is horizontal, if only for a heartbeat. Hogan scoops him up, muscles straining, the camera cutting just enough to hide the mechanics while preserving the illusion. The Silverdome erupts, and for a second the building itself seems to lift. In Hogan's account, he tore a biceps and hurt his back performing the slam. The move is not elegant; it is desperate, ugly, human. That's why it works. Perfection would have cheapened it. Effort sanctifies it.

After the slam comes the leg drop, almost as an afterthought, a procedural necessity. Hogan pins André, the referee counts, and history is declared. But the pin is not the climax. The climax was the lift, the moment when the rules of the universe appeared to bend. Everything after that is paperwork.

It is tempting to read the match as a simple allegory of American optimism, the triumph of will over circumstance, the small guy beating the big guy, even though Hogan was never the small guy in any meaningful sense. But that reading misses the sadness baked into the spectacle. André's loss was not just the end of a streak; it was the end of a way of being. André was an icon of a bygone era, the territorial era in pro wrestling when there were twenty different pro wrestling "realities" around the country at any given time. An era in which fantastical creatures like André the Giant roamed the earth, moving from territory to territory to find the next willing audience, and where the only notion a fan might have of André was from word of mouth or a photo in a black-and-white wrestling magazine. It felt like a permanent way of being at the time, until there came cable television and Vince McMahon and Hulk Hogan. André was the invulnerable, unknowable old school, and that establishment was being hoisted high in the sky in the Silverdome. The mountain had been moved, and in doing so, admitted it could be moved. There is a melancholy to that admission, a recognition that even the most protected myth eventually pays rent to reality.

WrestleMania III also marked a turning point in how wrestling understood itself. The event proved that wrestling could sell moments as effectively as matches, that a single image could anchor an entire industry. It validated the idea that wrestling's greatest currency was shared memory. People remember where they were when Hogan slammed André the way people remember where they were for moon landings or title-clinching home runs. Wrestling, often derided as fake, had found a way to make itself feel permanent.

In the years that followed, wrestling would chase that feeling with diminishing returns. Bigger stadiums, louder pyrotechnics, more elaborate stunts. Everyone wanted their own Silverdome moment, their own photograph that could stand in for an era. For its part, the WWF tried to repeat the moment between Hogan and André again and again in the following eighteen months. But moments are not scalable. They depend on timing, on bodies being in the right place at the right moment, on audiences being ready to believe. Hogan and André met at the exact intersection of need and possibility. Move the match a year earlier or later, and it loses some of its voltage.

There is also the uncomfortable truth that the match's power is inseparable from its artifice. The slam was possible *because* André allowed it, because wrestling is a collaboration disguised as conflict. But that does not diminish the moment so much as it clarifies it. Wrestling's magic lies in its honesty about effort even when the outcome is predetermined. Hogan still had to lift André. André still had to endure the fall. The pain was real, even if the story was scripted.

Watching the match now, with decades of context and a more skeptical eye, you can see the seams. You can see André's limitations, Hogan's theatrics, the camera angles doing their part. You can also see something else: two men giving their bodies to a story larger than themselves. André's body, failing and finite, becomes a vessel for a final act of wonder. Hogan's body, honed and heroic, pushed beyond its limitations, becomes a bridge between possibility and fulfillment.

On that night, maybe more than any other, Hulk Hogan mattered because he could sell the dream and embody the dreams of a population. WrestleMania III is less about who won than about what was proven. Wrestling proved it could create a communal myth that transcended its own mechanics. It proved that belief is not about ignorance but about consent. The crowd knew, on some level, that this was a show. They also knew, on a deeper level, that shows can matter.

The photographs endure because they capture that contradiction. Hogan's face is a mask of strain; André's body is a testament to trust. The image says: This is hard, and it is meaningful. That might be the most honest thing wrestling has ever said.

CHAPTER 5

THE BACKSTABBER

HULK HOGAN VS. FRIENDSHIP

Pro wrestling is a genre built on betrayal, but not all betrayals are created equal. Some are operatic—the sneak attack, the chair shot, the zombie stare. Others are intimate, almost petty, the kind that linger precisely because they feel human. The feud between Hulk Hogan and "Macho Man" Randy Savage, culminating at WrestleMania V, belongs squarely in the latter category. It is remembered as a clash of titans, but it was really about something smaller and more uncomfortable: friendship, insecurity, and the quiet realization that the American hero might actually be the villain. Hogan-Savage was not a feud born of ambition or ideology or mythology or geopolitics. It was born of anxiety.

The Mega Powers—Hogan and Savage's short-lived team moniker—were presented as an inextinguishable fire, two avatars of 1980s excess fused into one superteam. Hogan was the eternal sun, all arms and absolutes. Savage was the moon, volatile and obsessive, brilliant in short, explosive bursts. Together, they were unstoppable.

But the key to the story was always that they were never equals. Hogan did not need Savage, but Savage needed Hogan—he needed the validation that an association with Hogan brought, and he needed to believe that Hogan needed him. The feud works because it understands that imbalance, and then refuses to resolve it cleanly.

* * *

The received wisdom for decades was that Randy Savage was the paranoid one. The jealous champion. The unhinged egomaniac who couldn't handle sharing the spotlight. That interpretation is convenient, simple, and incomplete. Sure, the storyline's iconic promo was steeped in suspicion, but it wasn't wrong. "Behind my back," Savage warbled into the camera. "I loved you like a brother. I got proof right here. Yeah. You got lust in your eyes and in your black heart for Elizabeth." Miss Elizabeth was Savage's manager and girlfriend, who, in character, he thought Hogan was eyeing. (In real life they were married, and Savage was reportedly a disturbingly possessive and controlling partner.) Savage had reason to distrust Hogan, and the text supports him at every turn.

First, let us establish that Hogan—either due to Freudian error or an inability to evolve past the villainy of his early career—largely worked as a heel in the ring throughout his career. In the match in which he won the WWF title from the Iron Sheik—the defining moment of his rise to superstardom—he attacks the Sheik before the latter takes off his ring robe, attacks him with said robe, knees him in the neck, gouges his eyes, chokes him, and spits on him, all in the span of about two minutes. These are all signals of villainy, despite the fact that Hulk was supposed to be the hero.

People remember the high points of his set of moves: the "Hulking up," the finger wagging, the leg drop. But there were other standards: the illegal punch, the rake of the eyes, the rake of the back. Hogan's look may have been heroic, but much of his repertoire belonged to a rogue. The heel shtick extended beyond Hogan's ring work. Throughout his prime WWF period, between 1983 and 1993, Hogan was a jerk basically every moment that he wasn't boring. When he was beefing with over-the-top heels like Roddy Piper, Hogan looked knightly in relief. But when the dispute was an interpersonal one, Hogan almost always took the low road. Take the early example of his feud with "Mr. Wonderful" Paul Orndorff. It's often remembered as a simple heel turn, but it was really one of the first cracks in the Hulkamania myth—a preview of everything that would later curdle around Hogan's friendships.

When Orndorff turned heel on Hogan in 1986, the betrayal was presented as a shock, but the true revelation was that Orndorff had finally noticed something the audience had been conditioned to ignore: Being Hulk Hogan's friend was a dead end. Hogan and Orndorff were on-screen friends and sometime partners, until "Adorable" Adrian Adonis, wrestler and host of the *Flower Shop* interview segment, started needling Orndorff about his subordinate role in the relationship. Orndorff disputed the charge and insisted that if he called Hogan on the phone, he'd be right there to back him up. Moments later, during an ensuing match, Orndorff appears in an inset frame, trying in vain to get the Hulk on the phone. "I don't care what he's doin'!" he yells into the receiver. "I don't care that he's got 605 pounds on his back. You just go get him and tell him Mr. Wonderful wants to talk to him right now. Immediately!"

Hogan never returned the call. He was too busy working out. When they finally had a match, Hogan and Orndorff teaming against King Kong Bundy and Big John Studd, Orndorff seethed as Hogan ignored him throughout the match. His frustration grew and grew—it was a masterful acting performance—until he flipped, attacking Hogan and piledriving him. Orndorff took on Bobby Heenan (of course) as his new manager, and the heel turn was formalized. The final showdown between Hogan and Orndorff—at the Big Event on August 28, 1986, in Toronto—set attendance records. It's not hard to see how this feud was a trial run for Hogan's programs with André the Giant as well as Randy Savage. What Orndorff took exception to—and what André and Savage would realize as well—was that Hogan's friendship wasn't a two-way street, and no matter how selfishly he acted, Hogan would never not be the one getting cheers. Orndorff may have been jealous of Hogan's fame, but more poignantly he was exhausted by it. As "Mr. Wonderful," he was marketed at times as Hogan's equal, but the presentation never supported that idea. (Orndorff was inexplicably the star in the TV commercial for *Hulk Hogan's Hulkamania Workout Set*. Maybe Hogan was busy working out during the shoot.) Hogan soaked up the cheers, the camera angles, the moral authority. Orndorff stood next to him like a bodyguard who'd been promised a promotion that never came.

Every great villain in literature succeeds, in part, because they see themselves as the hero of the story. The brilliance of this feud is that Orndorff's grievance made sense. He didn't claim Hogan cheated him or sabotaged him outright. He accused Hogan of something worse: condescension. Hogan treated Orndorff the way he treated everyone—like a supporting character in the story of Hulk Hogan. Even worse, in a real-world sense it was true. Orndorff, Savage, André—all were high-wattage babyfaces whose heroism was sacrificed at the altar of Hulkamania. They were villains because Hogan's storyline required it. When Orndorff snapped, it felt less like a turn to the dark side than like self-respect finally curdling into rage.

Hogan's response was telling. He never examined his role in the fallout. He framed Orndorff's anger as betrayal, full stop—apostasy, a rejection of the new religion. The narrative demanded it, and Hogan's character couldn't allow for nuance. If someone turned on Hogan, they had to be in the wrong—and they had to be defeated. In retrospect, the Hogan-Orndorff feud reads like a warning label. Hulkamania thrived on loyalty, but rarely returned it.

* * *

Vince McMahon is cited as saying that fans have a short memory span. It's a lesson he must have learned by 1989, when he booked the Hogan-Savage feud as a straight cover of Hogan-Orndorff. The parallels are striking, but the most significant difference is the presence of Miss Elizabeth: wrestling's Helen of Troy, not your conventional meddling manager but rather a face at ringside that would launch a thousand dropkicks.

Elizabeth was presented as the object over which the men fought, not as a participant in the conflict. Her emotions were implied, not articulated. Her discomfort was visible, but rarely verbalized. She functioned as a moral mirror; whoever stood closest to her was presumed righteous. That made her one of the most powerful figures in wrestling history—and also one of the most constrained.

Elizabeth's presence humanized Savage. Without her, his intensity might have reverted back into villainy much sooner. With her, he became tragic rather than monstrous. She was the emotional ballast that made his jealousy legible. When Savage worried about Hogan's intentions, Elizabeth didn't roll her eyes or scold him. She looked torn. Concerned. Caught in the middle. In doing so, she quietly legitimized Savage's fears.

Historically, Elizabeth represents a turning point in pro wrestling's portrayal of women. She wasn't a pinup, a seductress, or a punchline. She was dignified, restrained, and emotionally resonant. The crowd cared about her not because she screamed or slapped people, but because she felt real in a genre that often didn't. That realism came at a cost. Elizabeth was rarely allowed to speak for herself. Her role was to react, not to decide. She mattered immensely, but mostly as a symbol. And yet, as with Hogan, symbols shape history. When she was the center of the drama in Savage's feuds, she was a more prestigious prize than a world championship.

The WWF World Heavyweight Championship, it should be noted, belonged to Savage after he won it at WrestleMania IV on March 22, 1988. It was taken from Hogan in a rematch between Hogan and André on *The Main Event* that went awry in any number of ways. André's guru, "The Million Dollar Man" Ted Dibiase, paid off referee Earl Hebner to secretly sub in for his twin brother, referee Dave Hebner (who was tied up backstage) and skew the match in André's favor. It worked—André got the pin, and Hebner counted to three despite Hogan's shoulder being off the mat—but when, after the match, André gifted the title to Dibiase, that was apparently a step too far—WWF president Jack Tunney vacated the title and made a tournament for it, which Savage won. (In reality, Hogan gave up the title because he was going off to film *No Holds Barred*.)

Little wonder that Hogan suddenly became invested in Savage's career at the moment when Savage took ownership of the belt. The two started teaming up, Savage started wearing red and yellow, and the arc toward their inevitable breakup began.

The crux of the dispute occurred on the February 2, 1989, episode of *The Main Event*, when the Mega Powers were set to face off against the Twin Towers, two villains that presumably bonded over their shared love for wrongdoing and all-you-can-eat buffets. They certainly didn't have a gimmick overlap—The Big Bossman was a correctional officer from Cobb County, Georgia, and Akeem the African Dream was a white dude in a dashiki and kufi (no capital) who pretended to be African (while loosely imitating Dusty Rhodes, superstar of the NWA, who was purported to be the target of the lampoon, not that any of the kids watching understood that at all).

Prior to the match, Hogan and Savage were interviewed backstage and Hogan was asked about why he referred to the Mega Powers as a "Triangle of Love." Things got uncomfortable quickly. "It's the love, man, that's gonna supercharge the Mega

Powers and tear down the Twin Towers. It's the love between me and Miss Elizabeth"—Savage recoiled at this line, but Hogan quickly recovered—"the love between a brother and a sister. It's the love between me and the Macho Man, the love between two brothers, between two partners, between two friends. And it's also the love between the Macho Man and Elizabeth, the way a man feels about a woman. When the Macho Man looks at Elizabeth, the way Elizabeth looks at him, it's like a radar beam, a laser beam stronger than the sun. It's love that will lead the Mega Powers to victory." Needless to say, this was the first time Hogan referenced any kind of love triangle—even a platonic one—in any of his major storylines.

The match got off to a good start, though heel commentator Jesse "The Body" Ventura couldn't help but notice that Hogan was reluctant to tag Savage in: "It's like Hogan's out for all the glory." On play-by-play, Vince McMahon pointed out that, well, he didn't need to tag Savage in—he was doing fine on his own, and even at home you can sense the tenuousness of this argument. It made it somehow worse that the voice of the heroes (McMahon) was making the case, because it was fairly obvious that Ventura was telling the truth. Eventually the match breaks down into a fracas, the Towers' manager Slick gets involved to turn the tide toward his team, and then, out of nowhere, Bossman tosses Savage outside the ring and onto an unsuspecting Miss Elizabeth, sending them both into a pile on the floor. Hogan rushes over to check on them, giving cursory attention to Savage as he stumbles to his feet. But the real attention—the awkwardly tender, overly touchy-feely kind of attention that does not at all speak to a brother-sister relationship—was saved for Elizabeth, who was on the floor, unconscious.

With Savage stuck in the ring getting pummeled by Bossman and Akeem, Hogan lifts Elizabeth in his arms, tears streaming down his face, and carries her down the aisle to a waiting gurney. They wheel Elizabeth into a medical room, where she is seen to by trainers while Hogan clutches her hand and prays out loud for God to save her. Note that the camera follows Hogan, even as the match proceeds. It was in the interest of the story, sure, but it didn't do away with the notion that Hogan was the main character and everyone else a mere costar. Elizabeth regains consciousness and pleads to Hogan to go back out and help Savage.

Hogan does—he returns to the match, pounding on the mat to announce his arrival (and draw attention to himself). Savage, who had spent the entire previous stanza getting whooped, doesn't tag Hogan in when he has the chance. It is only after he dumps both Towers out of the ring that he walks toward Hogan standing in the corner and dramatically slaps him in the face.

Savage leaves Hogan alone in the ring and decamps for the locker room. The camera stays with Hogan in the ring, naturally. Hogan goes on to win the match singlehandedly, naturally. When Hogan meets up with his loved ones backstage, Savage lays into him. "You're outta line! And let me tell you why you're outta line: You've got jealous eyes right there. Right there you're looking at me with jealous eyes, because you're a former champion. I was the one carrying you!" He insists that Hogan is too cowardly to ask him for a title shot, and then turns the knife as Hogan tries to talk him down: "Those eyes right there? Those eyes lust Elizabeth. You got lust for Elizabeth right there, and I'm gonna tell you it makes me sick. I can't even stand to look at you."

As Hogan begs Elizabeth to talk some sense into him, Savage

attacks Hogan, pummeling him on the floor. When Elizabeth tries to intervene, Savage tosses her away violently. I guess they had to put that into the script because up until that point, it was unclear who the villain was.

* * *

Through the years, on-screen and off, Hulk Hogan insists he's just being a good guy. In the most objectionable moments of his real life, Hogan seems to shrug his shoulders and wonder Job-like why he, the hero, is being put through such trials. On-screen, he has consistently been egocentric. Savage sees this, and Savage is right.

Pro wrestling is an uneasy space for friendships in general, as they more often than not turn into rivalries, but even in that world, Hogan is an especially lousy friend. He assumes moral authority by default, because that is what Hulk Hogan does. His entire character is built on the premise that his instincts are correct, his actions justified, and his presence inherently stabilizing. If something goes wrong, Hogan will fix it—whether or not anyone asked him to. That's not friendship. That's paternalism.

A good friend doesn't insert himself into your marriage and then act offended when you're upset about it. A good friend doesn't treat your personal boundaries as optional, especially when the power dynamic is this skewed. Hogan was the face of the company, the avatar of the WWF's moral universe. Savage was the champion, but Hogan was the main character. Everyone knew it. Especially Savage. Savage's paranoia wasn't madness. It was pattern recognition.

What their match at WrestleMania V ultimately exposed is the central contradiction of the Hogan character: He cannot exist in a world of equals. Hogan's persona works only if everyone else is either a villain or a beneficiary. You can be saved by Hogan. You can be defeated by Hogan. But you cannot truly stand beside Hogan without eventually being diminished. The spotlight bends toward him. The moral compass recalibrates around his choices. His goodness is not relational; it is absolute.

This is why the Mega Powers were always doomed. Savage's character was defined by intensity, insecurity, and emotional honesty. He felt things too much. Hogan's character was defined by emotional simplicity. He felt the right thing, at the right volume, at all times. When Savage expressed doubt or jealousy, the narrative framed it as weakness—even when the doubt was justified.

The WrestleMania V showdown was very good, but much less important than the blowup that preceded it. Hogan won, no surprise there. If anything, one is awed that the greatness of the match is undeniably Savage's doing. We had seen enough Hogan matches to know what portion of the credit was his, and this match far exceeded that mark. Looking back from a modern perspective—one shaped by a healthy dose of skepticism, the kind that probably fueled Savage's paranoia—the Hogan-Savage feud reads like an accidental critique of the very thing Hogan represented. It asks: What happens when the moral center of the universe refuses to acknowledge its own blind spots?

Hogan never apologizes. He never meaningfully reflects. Why would he? He always comes out on top. Savage got the WrestleMania spotlight, but he still came out feeling diminished, not because he lost the title but because he was forced to play second banana—and villain—to Hogan's star. Savage had worked night and day to raise himself to Hogan's stature; claiming the mantle of WWF champion during the Hogan era was an unimaginable feat, and the crowd loved him. But now he was a villain again because that's what it meant to stand across the ring from Hulk Hogan. That asymmetry is the tragedy of the story. WrestleMania V didn't just crown a champion. It exposed a fault line.

Savage was intense, volatile, and flawed—but he was honest about it. Hogan was confident, generous, and beloved—but incapable of seeing how his goodness could suffocate others. Hulk Hogan matters because he taught us that our heroes have flaws and blind spots, and that, in fact, they might not be heroes at all. He taught us a lesson that would predict the future; most of his career to that point had been about playacting the battles of our collective id. In 1989 he showed us that reality was stickier, that not every problem could be solved by leg dropping the meanest guy in the room. In a genre that thrives on clear heroes and villains, this feud dared to suggest something messier: that sometimes the worst harm is done by the person who thinks he can do no wrong. That's why the story endures. Not because of the match quality, or the spectacle, or even the championship. It endures because it feels true.

CHAPTER 6

THE TORCHBEARER

HULK HOGAN VS. THE ULTIMATE WARRIOR

Gorilla Monsoon repeatedly called the clash between WWF heavyweight champion Hulk Hogan and Intercontinental champ the Ultimate Warrior "the irresistible force versus the immovable object." It's an idiom you hear with some frequency, but it might come as a minor surprise to know that the phrase dates back to third-century China, in a book of Legalist philosophy called the *Han Feizi*, where there is a story about a merchant who says he has a spear that could pierce anything and a shield that could repel anything, and who is then confounded when someone asks him what would happen if he threw the spear at the shield.

The core idea is not about physics; it's about the logical paradox at play when two mutually exclusive ideas are somehow both true at the same time.

And that, oddly, describes the match between Hulk Hogan and the Ultimate Warrior match at WrestleMania VI better than even the face reading of the phrase. As a kid I always imagined both Hogan and Warrior as irresistible forces—that the phrase more aptly described Hogan-André than this matchup. But if the implication was that Warrior was the irresistible force—the undeniable, insurgent star—and Hogan was the immovable object—the mainstay, the permanent hero of the company—then Monsoon was deeply correct.

On paper, Hogan versus the Ultimate Warrior was pro wrestling distilled to its loudest primary colors: the immortal against the unstoppable, muscles stacked on muscles, face paint meeting tattered T-shirts, two action figures finally colliding in an arena big enough to justify the collision. It was billed as "The Ultimate Challenge," champion versus champion, a once-in-a-lifetime clash between the past and the future. And in the moment—inside Toronto's SkyDome, under the glow of a company still convinced it could make anything feel like the center of the universe—it worked. It felt like a coronation. But pro wrestling has a way of turning coronations into autopsies.

To understand Hogan versus Warrior, you have to remember what Hulk Hogan represented by 1990. He was the living proof of Vince McMahon's gamble that wrestling could be national, cartoonish, and moralistic all at once. Hogan's physique, his promos, his music, and even his enemies were carefully calibrated to fit McMahon's vision of a mainstream-friendly spectacle. Hogan didn't merely draw money—he justified the entire expansionist project. If Hogan had failed, the WWF would have likely failed with him.

By WrestleMania VI, though, Hogan was no longer new. He was reliable, durable, and increasingly familiar. The crowds still loved him, but the love had started to flatten into something more like habit. Sure, the crowds got bigger and bigger, but their reaction to Hogan hit maximum volume when he beat the Iron Sheik and André the Giant, and his career after 1987 was a never-ending quest to rediscover that high. Even as the WWF grew, the reaction to the first few power chords of Hogan's theme song was louder than the reaction after a Hogan win. We were in love with the phenomenon of Hulk Hogan, more so than the reality of him.

McMahon did his level best to keep Hogan interesting. Bigger and badder foes, as much mainstream crossover as they could find. But the problem with appealing to a mainstream audience as well as a younger demographic—Hogan's target audiences—is that you're constantly reintroducing the act to a new audience. There is no long-term narrative arc—Hulk Hogan existed in an ageless, radio serial kind of universe, where every feud hit the same beats, and always ended up the same. But longtime fans were getting restless; once you've seen him slam André, it's hard to get as excited about the next episode.

Enter the Ultimate Warrior: a star designed not to replace Hogan's message but to amplify it. Warrior was louder, less verbal, more feral. He didn't monologue; he roared. Where Hogan preached vitamins and prayers, Warrior promised annihilation. While Hogan paraded into the ring, hyping up the crowd, Warrior sprinted to the ring as if trying to fast-forward straight to the climax. He felt like what would happen if the Hogan formula were stripped of pretense and turned into pure motion.

The Ultimate Warrior, originally known as Jim Hellwig, had come to the WWF via the dwindling territorial system. He started off in Memphis as part of Powerteam USA, a crew of bodybuilders turned wrestlers, until he splintered off with fellow Powerteamer Steve Borden—later famously known as Sting—to form a tandem called the Freedom Fighters, later known as the Blade Runners. The face paint, the physiques, and the '80s action movie citation were all references to the iconic Road Warriors, the dominant tag team of the era. When they split up, Hellwig went to World Class Championship Wrestling in Dallas and renamed himself the Dingo Warrior. Like Hogan before him, he was electric enough there to defy his positioning as a villain, and became a star for the promotion just in time for Vince McMahon to come in and steal him away. Conscious of the Road Warrior reference, the WWF boldly renamed him the Ultimate Warrior, and as soon as he appeared in the WWF, he felt like a possible successor to Hogan. More than that—it felt like anything was possible. That made him dangerous.

* * *

The Ultimate Warrior's early entire WWF career could be distilled down to a minute-long highlight reel. There was him defeating Honky Tonk Man for the Intercontinental title in thirty-one seconds. There was the Super Posedown with Rick Rude. There was the Survivor Series match where he tossed André out of the ring. There were a lot of squash matches, and a lot of possessed, warbling promos. The entire three years from his first appearance in the WWF to his match against Hogan formed a carefully scripted arc, though it's hard to say if it was the WWF's scripting that made him the star that he was or whether they were just riding shotgun to the inevitability of Warrior's thrall, trying to hone and target an irresistible force.

The 1992 Royal Rumble is the first moment that brings Warrior and Hogan together. Every year, the Rumble has thirty men in the ring, entering one at a time and staying in until they're tossed over the top rope, so you never know who will cross paths with whom. This night, Warrior enters the match at number 21 and Hogan at 25. When they finally find themselves alone in the ring, the crowd lights up. They bump chests in cartoon antagonism. They take turns trying to knock each other down. They run the ropes and clothesline one another. It is a stalemate. It is a logical paradox. Eventually Warrior is eliminated when Hogan throws himself into Rick Rude and the Barbarian, who are trying to toss Warrior out. Warrior reenters the match illegally, clocks both the heels, and then sprints comically back up the aisle, leaving Hogan unscathed, and allowing him to win the Rumble.

The rapture of the crowd to the Ultimate Warrior's antics presaged Hogan's eventual loss. When they met in the ring, you could see the age on Hogan's face. His body looked roughly the same as it always had, but his face was puffier, lined, his hair unruly. Maybe it's just the juxtaposition with the Warrior, but standing across from his usurper, Hogan actually *looks* like a man at the end of his run. Before he just felt that way.

Aside from the Rumble moment, the feud—if that's even the word for it—was notably thin. There was mutual respect, some flexing, a few intense stare-downs, and not much else. No betrayal, no philosophical divide. Like Warrior's sprint to the ring, they fast-forwarded through all the boring parts, leaving only the assumption of a match based on the feeling of inevitability. Just two titans circling each other because eventually, the business demands that the biggest stars collide. Maybe they didn't need anything else, maybe their stars were so big that minimalism was called for. Because in retrospect, that thinness is revealing. McMahon wanted the match to feel epic rather than personal. If it went deeper, one of them would have had to be cast as the antagonist; André and Savage proved that this was a step backward, and perhaps uncertain of the long-term plan, McMahon couldn't afford for either man to lose steam. But it was a story about destiny, and as such, one man would have to give way so the other could move forward. And Hogan, crucially, was the one doing the giving.

The match at WrestleMania VI is often remembered fondly, if vaguely. The crowd was molten. Every move felt gigantic. When Warrior finally pinned Hogan clean in the middle of the ring, it was shocking precisely because it was so unambiguous. No cheating. No controversy. Hogan even lingered afterward, handing Warrior the belt and offering a long, searching look that suggested approval tinged with something harder to name. Regret, maybe. Or calculation.

In wrestling mythology, this was the passing of the torch. In wrestling reality, it was more like a loan.

The idea of the "passing of the torch" assumes that power transfers cleanly, that the old star steps aside and the new one takes over the role, the responsibilities, and the gravitational pull. But Hogan versus Warrior exposed a deeper truth about the WWF in that era: The torch wasn't Hogan's alone to pass. It belonged to Vince

McMahon. And McMahon had never been particularly good at letting go.

Once he took hold of the world title, Warrior's reign on top revealed the limits of both performers. Warrior had the look, the intensity, and the immediate crowd response, but he lacked Hogan's instincts for sustaining a character week after week. Hogan knew how to modulate himself, how to lose just enough heat to avoid backlash, how to recalibrate when the audience shifted. Warrior burned hot and fast. His promos were unhinged in a way that thrilled at first and exhausted soon after, and his matches were exciting but rote. He was a peak, not a plateau. It almost seemed that Warrior inadvertently leaned into every aspect of Hogan's act that was making him feel stale, and turned the volume up to 11. He was not the solution to a theoretical Hulk Hogan problem—he was just a purer distillation of it. The Ultimate Warrior experience was like mainlining Hulkamania—same drug, higher intensity, worse hangover.

Warrior was, for that moment, the new face of the WWF, but the central question that his reign raised had nothing at all to do with him. It was more primeval, at least in terms of WWF lore, even if the question was asked by accident: Who needed the other more—Hulk Hogan or Vince McMahon?

For years, the answer seemed obvious. Hogan needed McMahon's platform, his marketing machine, his belief in spectacle, and McMahon needed Hogan's star power. But WrestleMania VI complicates that story. Hogan didn't just accept defeat; he endorsed it. His willingness to lose cleanly wasn't altruism—it was leverage. By demonstrating that he could step aside and still remain Hogan, he proved his indispensability. Warrior could become the new champion, but he could never be the new Hulk Hogan. The company could try to move on, but it would do so in Hogan's shadow.

McMahon, meanwhile, learned a familiar lesson: Creating a star is easier than replacing one. Warrior needed the Hogan complicity to reach the summit, but the company still needed Hogan's stability once Warrior got there. Within a year, Hogan was back in the title picture, and Warrior's aura had already begun to fray. The torch hadn't been passed so much as briefly shared, then quietly reclaimed.

And this is where Hogan's real power becomes clear. Hogan controlled not just his victories but his losses. In wrestling, that's everything. To lose well is to dictate the narrative of your own decline. Hogan never allowed himself to become obsolete. Even when he lost, he framed the loss as part of a larger story in which he remained central. Warrior beat Hogan, but Hogan validated Warrior. Without Hogan's endorsement the win would have meant less. With it, Hogan stayed relevant by design. In a sense, the real-world lens is more instructive here than it was with Hogan's misguided attempt to retroactively validate his match with André. If you take it for granted that wrestling is fixed, then Hogan's loss at WrestleMania VI is more impressive than a win. He did what was best for the business—even if he knew what he was doing all along.

In that sense, WrestleMania VI wasn't about elevating the Ultimate Warrior. It was about reaffirming Hulk Hogan's role as the axis around which everything turned. Hogan could lose because losing didn't diminish him. It enhanced his myth. He was generous enough to step aside, strong enough to come back, and savvy enough to know that the business would eventually circle back to him.

The tragedy—or inevitability—of the Hogan-Warrior feud is that it promised a future the company wasn't structurally prepared to support. The WWF in 1990 didn't know how to live without Hogan at the center. McMahon's creative instincts, promotional strategies, and moral narratives were all built around one man. The Ultimate Warrior was a spectacular variation, not a foundational rewrite. And when the variation stopped working, the original was still there.

Looking back, the match stands as both a pinnacle and a warning. It's remembered because it felt big, clean, and decisive in a way wrestling rarely allows itself to be. But it also exposes the limits of wrestling's favorite metaphor. A torch doesn't pass itself. Someone has to hold it. Someone has to decide when to let it go. And someone has to be willing to take it back when the fire starts to sputter.

Hulk Hogan matters because he understood that better than anyone. He inherently grokked the business of pro wrestling almost instinctively; there would be limits to his philosophy, but his confidence was key to his power. WrestleMania VI wasn't the end of his era; it was proof that his era could survive even its own supposed ending. And that, more than any title belt, was the real victory. A loss and a victory at the same time; now, *that's* a paradox.

CHAPTER 7

THE SQUATTER

HULK HOGAN VS. MONOTONY

The problem with Hulk Hogan in the early 1990s wasn't that he stopped being a star. It was that he never stopped being Hulk Hogan. By 1990, the character had hardened into something immovable, a piece of cultural infrastructure rather than a living performer. As a kid, I hoped that the Hulkster would never lose. By the late '80s I quietly hoped that he would. By 1991, I knew he never would. Not really, anyway. He was no longer reacting to wrestling's gravity; gravity bent around him. The industry had changed, the audience had changed, the company had changed—and Hogan, stubbornly and profitably, refused to.

That refusal defined the strange, transitional chapter of Hogan's career after his loss to the Ultimate Warrior at WrestleMania VI through his quiet, awkward departure from the WWF and eventual reemergence in WCW. These were the years when Hulkamania stopped being the future and started being a burden. They were also the years when fans stopped pretending that its biggest star could exist outside the consequences of time, taste, and testimony. This is not the story of a downfall so much as a slow recalibration—one that Hogan resisted at every step, and one the WWF tried desperately to delay.

When Hogan lost the WWF Championship to the Ultimate Warrior, it was supposed to mean something profound. The torch-passing was literalized in the postmatch image: Hogan offering the belt to Warrior, Warrior lifting it with both hands like a trophy he wasn't quite sure how to carry. The symbolism was clean, even if the execution wasn't. Hogan was the past; Warrior was the future.

Except Hogan didn't go anywhere. The match itself was not a burial. Hogan lost clean, yes, but the aura stayed intact. The cameras lingered on him afterward, milking the moment, letting the audience process the idea of Hogan as something other than champion. But the company never committed to the idea that Hogan was done. This wasn't Flair losing to Sting or Terry Funk taking his body apart in Japan, where defeat was allowed to feel cumulative and final, where the wear and tear became part of the story. Hogan didn't lose that way. His defeats were never endpoints; they were pauses. He could give you a loss but not a conclusion. The WWF didn't present Hogan as a man moving toward the end of something—only as a star briefly stepping aside before reclaiming the center.

Within months, the question wasn't whether Hogan would reclaim the title but when.

This is the first key to understanding Hogan's early-'90s run: Defeat did not equal diminishment. Hogan had trained the audience—and Vince McMahon—too well for that. The Hulk Hogan of 1990 was less a wrestler than a setting. You didn't write him out; you worked around him.

* * *

The Ultimate Warrior's reign collapsed within nine months, undone by backstage distrust, creative uncertainty, and his own inability to carry the company the way Hogan had. Hogan, meanwhile, stayed conspicuously close to the main event. Even his absences were headline events.

When Hulk's music hit on May 26, 1990, kids in the arena jumped out of their seats, even though they knew Hogan wasn't going to wrestle. He was making an appearance on *The Brother Love Show*, the heir to *Piper's Pit* as the WWF's preeminent interview show, this one hosted by "Brother Love," a red-faced televangelist-slash–wrestling manager portrayed by Bruce Prichard, a backstage producer and close confidant of Vince McMahon. Hogan, having not learned his lesson about these talk show segments yet, came onto the stage and played to the crowd. He turned to take the microphone from Brother Love, but Love yanked it away and introduced his *second* guest, the Earthquake.

Earthquake's music hits but only his manager, "The Mouth of the South" Jimmy Hart, appears from the tunnel. He says that Earthquake has a fever and a sore throat and couldn't make it today.

Hogan, anticipating an opportunity to give Earthquake a piece of his mind, is angry; he grabs Hart by the lapels and demands he go get him. Hart—who, in real life, is one of Hogan's closest friends—starts laying into Hulk with some shocking honesty: "Keep your hands off me, you has-been! You're not the world champion anymore! You're nothing!"

Then, with surprising speed for a 400-plus-pound former sumo wrestler, Earthquake runs out from the back and hits Hogan with a folding chair. He taunts Hogan and then flattens him with what was then the most terrifying move in wrestling (and, for what it's worth, maybe the most *legitimately* terrifying), the Earthquake Splash, which consisted of Earthquake, an enormously fat fellow, running up, jumping, and dropping himself butt-first onto his prone opponent's chest. The move—a variation on the classic seated senton—was so well executed, it looked like attempted murder. He plants Hogan with a second Splash, then a third.

A mob of WWF officials come running out from the back to pull Earthquake off him and then tend to Hogan. A ringside doctor is with them, and after checking Hogan's pulse and eyes, he waves his hand in the air to call it. "Get him on the stretcher!" The faces of terrified kids in the crowd begin to chant in unison: "Hogan! Hogan!"

There are probably ten or twelve WWF officials on the scene but, almost comically, they can't figure out how to work together to lift Hogan.

Then, from out of nowhere, Vince McMahon appears, stripping off his blazer as he squeezes in to help them lift Hulk. "Come on! Get him out of here!" It's impossible to tell if Vince here is in character (as the play-by-play announcer running over to help) or out of character (as the boss trying to hurry things along). His angst and urgency suggest the latter. There were always jokes about Vince owning the company, but to the public he was presented as the announcer, never as the owner. It wasn't until much later that he would transform into an on-screen evil owner-*character*. Now he was caught somewhere in between.

❋ ❋ ❋

The most important rivalry of Hulk Hogan's 1980s career never took place in a ring. It unfolded instead backstage, in offices, and in the unspoken negotiations over who, exactly, the World Wrestling Federation belonged to. Maybe it only existed in the minds of fans or nosy onlookers, but by all accounts it was a going concern even in the heyday of the WWF. Publicly, Vince McMahon and Hulk Hogan were inseparable: promoter and champion, visionary and vessel. Privately, their relationship began as a close friendship and allegiance, had evolved into a low-grade cold war over authorship—over whether the WWF's success flowed *through* Hogan or *from* McMahon.

Hogan believed, with some justification, that he *was* the WWF. House show attendance rose and fell with his presence. Merchandising exploded around his image. When he was off the road, business dipped. The fans didn't chant "WWF." They chanted "Hogan." In the pro-Hogan view, Vince McMahon didn't create Hulkamania; he merely filmed it.

McMahon, of course, saw it differently. The WWF wasn't a star—it was a system. Hogan was the most successful expression of that system but still replaceable, in theory, if not immediately in practice. Vince had watched other promotions collapse after mistaking popularity for infrastructure. He wasn't going to let his company be held hostage by any one performer, no matter how profitable.

This philosophical divide manifested in subtle but telling ways. Hogan's contracts were lucrative but never permanent. His creative input was respected but never absolute. McMahon constantly tested the boundaries of Hogan's indispensability—experimenting with alternatives like Randy Savage and the Ultimate Warrior, teasing life after Hogan long before Hogan was willing to imagine it himself.

To Hogan, these experiments felt like betrayal. He had given McMahon legitimacy, national visibility, and cultural relevance. He had carried the company through expansion, through risk, through moments where failure would have been catastrophic. The tension wasn't about money alone (though money certainly played a part; there is no retirement plan for ex-champions); it was about narrative ownership. Hogan wanted to be remembered as the engine of the boom. McMahon wanted history to show that the boom was an inevitable result of his vision—that Hulkamania was brilliant casting, not a shared act of creation.

This rivalry explains much of Hogan's behavior in the early 1990s. His reluctance to fully step aside. His insistence on protected losses. His tendency to reassert himself just as the company tried to move past him. Hogan wasn't only fighting younger wrestlers; he was fighting erasure. Every comeback was a reminder to McMahon that the WWF's greatest era had a face, and it was his.

The Earthquake angle was instructive. Hogan sold vulnerability in a way that suggested mortality without ever quite embracing it. He was injured, yes, but only so he could return stronger, more righteous, more inevitable. The message was subtle but clear: Hogan might fall, but he would never fade. This was the paradox the WWF couldn't escape. Hogan was no longer the unquestioned face of the future, but he was still the safest investment the company had. Every attempt to move past him came with a contingency plan that involved bringing him back.

His following feud with Sgt. Slaughter, who had gone from being an All-American veteran to an Iraqi sympathizer during the height of the US-Iraq conflict in 1991, was, if nothing else, evidence that the wrestling world had grown uncomfortable with the simple jingoism of the '80s. Hogan, the red-blooded American avatar, was the obvious foil for Slaughter—who had dispossessed the Ultimate Warrior from the championship—and a fairly neat parallel to the Iron Sheik in terms of being a transitional champion whose value rested solely in geopolitical outrage. But this did not work as the Sheik angle did; maybe values shifted, maybe the amount of stage time they gave Slaughter to offend the audience made it obvious that the WWF was complicit in the anti-Americanism. But regardless, interest in Hogan-Slaughter was minimal. They moved the event from the 100,000-seat Los Angeles Memorial Coliseum to the 15,000-seat Los Angeles Memorial Sports Arena next door due to low ticket sales. The WWF claimed (and claims) that threats to Slaughter's life were the reason for the move, but there were not 100,000 people outraged enough to buy a ticket to see him get his comeuppance, and that had always been proof of concept in the world of pro wrestling.

The response to Hogan was similarly muted. He won the WWF

Championship from Slaughter at WrestleMania VII, reclaiming his spot at the top, and the crowd response was tepid, and not just because of the number of seats. They were not hostile but cautious. Hogan was still beloved, but the temperature had changed. The audience was no longer a single mass chanting in unison; it was beginning to fragment.

Hogan's feud with The Undertaker later that year was one of the most intriguing of this era. The Undertaker was a new star, a zombie Old West mortician whose oddity and brutality had made him a fast-rising star. At Survivor Series 1991, The Undertaker defeated Hogan for the WWF Championship in a match designed to protect Hogan more than elevate Undertaker. The finish muddied the waters just enough to justify an immediate rematch. While Undertaker's manager, Paul Bearer, distracted the referee, Ric Flair, the longtime star of rival company WCW, ran to ringside and slid a steel chair into the ring. 'Taker piledrove Hogan onto the chair. In real life, Hogan had warned the Undertaker that he had a neck injury and that he was wary of taking that move, so 'Taker cinched it up and as a result hit him with one of the worst-looking Tombstone piledrivers of all time, with Hogan's head a good half foot away from the chair when 'Taker's knees hit the ground. The Undertaker won the match; despite the lack of contact, Hogan claimed backstage that he had been legitimately injured by the move. It was a political ploy by Hogan to hurt the credibility of his young rival.

Until the end of his life, Hogan insisted that the injury was real, despite the fact that easily accessible video disproved it. It was like the André finish—a lie for the sake of protecting his character's imaginary credibility.

The rematch came six days later, when Hogan regained the title from The Undertaker. The message was unmistakable. The Undertaker could beat Hogan—but only temporarily, and only with caveats. This was the pattern Hogan established in the early '90s: elevate without surrendering. He gave rubs, not reigns. The future could touch the belt, but Hogan would take it back.

Speaking of Flair—his feud with Hogan should have been a legendary moment in time, but Vince McMahon never let it happen. Flair was the face of the NWA/WCW, the traveling champion, the work-rate king, the man who defined excellence through excess. Hogan was the immovable center, the icon whose very presence simplified storytelling. Their rivalry should have been generational. Instead, their planned clash at WrestleMania VIII was shelved and the WWF went with Flair vs. Savage and Hogan vs. Sid Justice. Justice was the latest in the line of "next Hogans," and Hogan won their match via disqualification, a supremely disappointing ending to a WrestleMania main event and the latest in the series of avoidable disappointments for Hogan. He had meddled in his feud with The Undertaker, somehow avoided a match with Flair, and worked his replacement to a draw. He wouldn't risk relinquishing the spotlight here as he had with Warrior. From this point onward, the stories of Hogan's politicking and strong-arming became the stuff of legend.

Vince and Hogan had competing priorities, but their passive aggression was in sync, and the reign of Hulkamania limped onward with no resolution, every Hogan win another month of life support for the dwindling regime. In that way it's feasible that the two men were perhaps even more inextricable at the end than they were at the beginning.

A year later, Hogan made another return to the title picture at WrestleMania IX. It was supposed to be a feel-good moment. Instead, it became a case study in creative dissonance. After Bret Hart—the latest in the string of Hogan replacements—lost the WWF Championship to Yokozuna, Hogan emerged unexpectedly to defend Bret—and, ever the terrible friend, ended up accepting a match against Yokozuna. The match was brief, one-sided, and designed to put the belt back on Hogan without explanation or justification.

In the process, Bret Hart—the company's newly chosen champion—was sidelined, his victory erased, his momentum disrupted. Hogan didn't just win the title; he overrode the plan. This moment encapsulated Hogan's late-WWF problem. He was still powerful enough to change the narrative simply by appearing. But that power came at the expense of the future the company was trying to build.

Hogan's final WWF feud with Yokozuna was short, strange, and symbolic. He lost the WWF Championship back to Yokozuna in Japan, away from the American spotlight, in a match that should have been a climax and instead felt like a quiet concession. There was no grand farewell. No emotional speech. No acknowledgment that an era was ending. Hogan simply left. Maybe since he always came back, it felt unnecessary.

For the last half decade of his WWF tenure, Hulk Hogan existed in a state of productive denial. He denied age, denied diminishing returns, denied the idea that wrestling could thrive without him at the center. The WWF found it impossible to truly separate itself from that denial because it was profitable, because it was familiar, and because it delayed harder decisions.

When Hogan finally left, it wasn't because he failed—it was because the business could no longer pretend that success looked the same as it had in 1987. Or rather, it was because the WWF could no longer pretend it *was* 1987. In some sense, Hulk Hogan mattered at that moment less than he ever had, but he clearly mattered to McMahon. As much as he tried to move past him, he couldn't ever fully commit to it.

Hogan didn't fall. He outlasted his own context. And in doing so, he taught the industry a lesson it would spend the rest of the decade trying to unlearn: Eventually, even the biggest star has to make room for the future—or become its obstacle.

CHAPTER 8

THE LIAR

HULK HOGAN VS. STEROIDS

Professional wrestling is a business built on lies, which is another way of saying it's built on belief. You know the outcomes are predetermined, you know the angles are cooked, and yet you still find yourself caring deeply about who is strong, who is wronged, and who deserves one last shot. No one has lived more comfortably inside that contradiction than Hulk Hogan, a man whose career was essentially a decades-long case study in how confidence can alchemize exaggeration into accepted truth.

Hogan didn't just lie the way wrestlers lie—inside the ring, for the sake of a story. He lied the way people lie when they've spent so long playing a character that the character starts freelancing in real life. His lies weren't usually malicious or strategic. They were expansive. Improvisational. They sprawled. And in their sprawl, they revealed something fundamental about both Hogan and the culture that made him.

Start with the simplest category: the tall tales. Hogan has, at various points, claimed that Elvis Presley was a Hulkamaniac, that he partied with John Belushi in Los Angeles, that Metallica wanted him to play bass, that the Rolling Stones wanted him to play bass, that George Foreman stole the George Foreman grill from him, and that he was offered the lead role in *The Wrestler* before it went to Mickey Rourke. These lies are funny because they're unnecessary, but also because they're so bald-faced. Belushi and Presley were both dead by the time Hogan says he encountered them. The rest have been met with utter confusion from the other parties involved. The oddest part is that Hogan felt the need to tell the lies at all. Hogan didn't need Elvis or Metallica. He was *Hulk Hogan*. He lived a singularly spectacular life, but he was compelled to embellish nonetheless.

That instinct carried over into wrestling history itself. Hogan has consistently overstated his importance to virtually every major development in the industry, even when the truth would already paint him as indispensable. He didn't just help make WrestleMania a success; he was the sole reason it worked. He didn't just play a role in wrestling's boom periods; he *was* the boom. Everyone else—promoters, opponents, entire locker rooms—were supporting characters in the Hogan Cinematic Universe.

Nowhere is this more obvious than in his interactions with other wrestlers. Hogan has often framed his matches as acts of generosity, moments where he single-handedly elevated opponents by allowing them to share oxygen with him. In this telling, Randy Savage didn't become a megastar because of his own charisma and volatility; he became one because Hogan picked him from obscurity and allowed him to flourish. The Ultimate Warrior didn't beat Hogan at WrestleMania VI because the company was moving on; Hogan personally carved Warrior's face on Mount Rushmore. Even losses became a form of dominance, because they were reframed as gifts.

There's a truth to some of this, as I have discussed; Hogan had the backstage power to affect the careers of others to a significant degree. But his lies fly in the face even of that reality. He insisted that he was never political, never manipulative, never concerned with protecting his spot. This is the most revealing lie of all, because it contradicts observable reality in a way that borders on performance art. Hogan didn't just play backstage politics; he *lived* backstage politics. He understood leverage, optics, and timing better than almost anyone of his era. He knew when to attach himself to hot acts, when to veto finishes, when to quietly steer creative away from threats. He seemed to genuinely believe that politicking didn't count as politics, because in his mind they were simply common sense. Gravity isn't political, and neither, the thinking goes, was Hulk Hogan winning.

For years, these lies thrived. Wrestling rewarded them. Wrestling needed them. The business depended on larger-than-life certainty, on men who could speak in absolutes and make the impossible feel righteous. Hogan was the perfect avatar for that system. He told you who he was, what he stood for, and why it mattered, loudly enough that doubt felt like bad manners.

Then the context changed.

In 1991, the World Wrestling Federation found itself colliding with a reality it couldn't simply no-sell. Dr. George Zahorian, a Pennsylvania physician who had worked as a ringside doctor for the WWF (when such roles were mandated by state sports overseers), was convicted of illegally supplying steroids to clients, including WWF wrestlers, and packages of them were sent to Vince McMahon's office at WWF headquarters. A federal investigation into steroid distribution and usage eventually crystallized into *The United States vs. McMahon*, known commonly as the WWF steroid trial, which dragged pro wrestling into a national conversation about performance-enhancing drugs, masculinity, and accountability.

And at the center of that storm was Hogan, not just as a witness but as a symbol. His body had been wrestling's most effective marketing tool for a decade. Now it was evidence. The problem wasn't that fans suddenly discovered steroids existed; everyone already knew. Steroids themselves weren't illegal until November 1990, when the Anabolic Steroids Control Act was passed, which is often forgotten in the relitigation of this period. The problem was that this trial wasn't really about guilt or innocence so much as exposure. It forced wrestling to explain itself to people who didn't understand it. And wrestling's biggest star was being asked to stop winking and start testifying.

Hogan lied his way all the way to the stand. He was given immunity by the prosecution to testify against Vince McMahon. Hogan said he would, right up until he got on the stand. Once there, he did an about-face and said Vince had never distributed steroids or even suggested that he take them. The judge dismissed the distribution charge and the jury acquitted McMahon on the charge of conspiracy. Exiting the court in a foam neck brace—which prompted a lot of people to think he was trying to invoke some sort of sympathy from the jury, though McMahon says that was not the case—Vince proudly declared his innocence. But he was still beaten in the eyes of much of the public. There were other issues, too, that changed the perception of the WWF: Former WWF referee Rita Chatterton accused McMahon of sexual assault; there were allegations that the young men ("ring boys") the WWF employed to help set up the ring were victims of systematic sexual abuse by WWF employees. McMahon denied these claims and was never found guilty of any wrongdoing, and Hogan was not named in either of those cases, but as the face of the industry, his reputation took a blow.

The worst damage had been done by his own hand. Hogan appeared on *The Arsenio Hall Show* in 1991, after Zahorian was arrested but three years before the trial, and claimed he'd only used steroids "once or twice." It was so absurd that it hardly feels like the same category as the other lies. Hogan delivered it with the calm confidence of a man used to controlling the narrative, smiling and nodding like a parent explaining a youthful indiscretion. Just like always, he assumed he would tell a lie and everything would be okay.

But the lie collided with something Hogan had never really had to contend with before: visual reality. His body told a different story. This wasn't a minor exaggeration or a fuzzy memory. It was a claim that actively insulted the audience's eyes. Wrestling fans, long trained to accept the impossible inside the ring, drew a line when the impossible was presented as mundane truth. You can believe in a leg drop as a finishing move. You can't believe in decades of obvious enhancement explained away as a brief experiment.

What made the moment linger wasn't just the dishonesty; it was the miscalculation. Arsenio Hall's audience wasn't hostile, but it was culturally literate. This was a show built on rhythm, irony, and the idea that authenticity mattered even when performance was part of the deal. Hogan answered like he was cutting a promo—polished, rehearsed, hollow—and the disconnect was palpable. For the first time, the Hulkster felt out of step with the culture he once towered over.

The effect wasn't immediate exile. Hogan didn't vanish. He didn't stop drawing money. But something subtly shifted. The belief changed shape. Fans began to separate Hulk Hogan the character from Terry Bollea the man, and the gap between them grew harder to ignore. If he was willing to lie so casually about something so obvious, what else had been exaggerated, reframed, or quietly erased?

This is where Hogan's lies stopped being charming and started being revealing. The same instinct that once turned a middling match into an epic now worked to sand down moral edges. Apologies came with explanations. Accountability came diluted by context. Hogan always seemed less interested in reckoning than in recalibrating the story until it felt survivable.

Ironically, the reinvention that would follow—Hollywood Hogan, the black-and-white, the sneer—worked because it leaned into that fracture. It acknowledged, even if indirectly, that the old sincerity was gone. But Hogan would later retell even that transformation as another act of singular genius, another inevitability only he could see coming. Even change itself had to orbit him.

What makes all of this fascinating, rather than simply exhausting, is that Hogan's lies worked for as long as they did because wrestling wanted them to. The business thrives on exaggerated truth. It rewards people who can say something with such conviction that it feels real even when it isn't. Hogan was wrestling's most successful illusionist. His lies reassured audiences that everything was bigger, better, and more meaningful than it actually was. Hulk Hogan mattered immensely to that era of pro wrestling, and his lies were the fuel that made it work. Eventually he would come to matter more as a different sort of avatar: the symbol of everything wrong with the business.

Hogan kept cutting promos in interviews up until his death, convinced that if he just added one more detail, one more famous name, one more heroic framing, the story will lock into place. It never did.

But the lies endure, stacked on top of one another like championship belts in an epic career. They tell you exactly who Hulk Hogan thought he was, and who professional wrestling once needed him to be. In a business built on worked realities, that might be the truest thing he ever offered.

CHAPTER 9

THE HACK

HULK HOGAN VS. HOLLYWOOD

Hulk Hogan did not become an actor because he possessed latent thespian gifts crying out for discovery. He became an actor because, at a certain point in American pop culture, Hulk Hogan became unavoidable. Acting was not so much a career pivot as it was magnetism doing its thing. When you are six foot seven, bronzed like a Thanksgiving turkey, wrapped in yellow and red like a human hazard sign, and capable of selling out arenas by flexing and ripping cotton asunder, Hollywood eventually wanders over and asks for your number.

Hogan's acting career is best understood not as a traditional filmography but as an extended experiment in brand extension. This was not about range, or character, or even credibility. This was about figuring out how much Hulkamania could survive once it left the ring and wandered into places where the choreography was looser, the dialogue was to be delivered in anything other than a growl, and the audience could not be distracted by a well-timed big boot.

Wrestling, at its peak, is a live-action morality play where subtlety is a bug, not a feature. Hogan was surely the Laurence Olivier of that stage. He pointed, he posed, he listened to the crowd. His genius—because it was a kind of genius—was understanding that realism was irrelevant. Emotion was the product. Everything else was scaffolding.

Movies, unfortunately, care about scaffolding.

* * *

Rocky III is the outlier, the ringer on Hogan's résumé, the one time you can say, with a straight face, "He was perfect for that part." Hogan's role as Thunderlips (inspired by the boxer-versus-wrestler match between Chuck Wepner and André the Giant at Shea Stadium on June 25, 1976) is essentially a wrestling cameo elevated to mythic absurdity. He is not asked to act so much as to incarnate. Thunderlips is wrestling's self-image as seen through a Hollywood funhouse mirror: enormous, cartoonish, faintly menacing, and not especially concerned with the emotional stakes of the story happening around him.

This is important, because Hogan is at his best when the movie understands exactly what it has hired. Thunderlips does not need inner conflict. He needs to look like he could kill Sylvester Stallone by accident, which Hogan accomplishes simply by standing there, flexing, and vibrating with the kind of confidence normally associated with generals and game show hosts.

The brilliance of *Rocky III* is that it frames Hogan correctly—not as the protagonist or even the antagonist, but as a natural disaster with a robe and top hat. His performance works because the movie never asks him to do anything smaller than his silhouette. He is pure spectacle, a living metaphor for the artificiality of pro wrestling contrasted with Rocky's blue-collar pugilism.

Hogan didn't have to act. He had to exist. This distinction matters, because it will be ignored for the rest of his career.

* * *

No Holds Barred is what happens when Hulk Hogan the brand gets full creative license and Hulk Hogan the actor is asked to carry a movie on charisma alone. This is a mission statement carved into granite with a jackhammer, under the guise of a motion picture.

In it, Hogan plays Rip, a wrestler so virtuous that his moral clarity could power a small city. Rip is everything Hogan wanted Hogan to be in the late '80s: righteous, indestructible, beloved by children, and perpetually persecuted by shadowy forces who hate freedom, muscles, or America itself. Indeed, Hogan co-wrote the part himself, along with Vince McMahon; they cooped up in a hotel room and wrote the whole movie in two and a half days. It shows.

The movie is more interested in validation than narrative. Every scene is designed to confirm that Rip—and by extension Hogan—is correct, heroic, and morally superior to anyone who questions him. It also attempts to validate Hogan as a crossover star, as if to shout "who needs Hollywood when you're a superstar?" This is where Hogan's limitations as an actor become impossible to ignore. In wrestling, you can pause. You can flex. You can let the crowd do half the work. In movies, silence reads as emptiness. Hogan fills that emptiness the only way he knows how: by turning every emotion into a catchphrase and every line reading into a declaration of purpose.

Subtlety is not just absent here; it is actively shunned. Hogan delivers dialogue like he's trying to reach the back row of an arena that isn't there. His facial expressions are either grin, scowl, or the transitional state between the two. Emotional nuance never enters the building.

Yet—and this is important—*No Holds Barred* works as a cultural artifact because it is so nakedly sincere. Hogan believes in Rip with the fervor of a man defending a constitutional amendment. There is no irony, no wink, no self-awareness. If Hogan ever comprehended the implicit outrageousness of his full-time job, it doesn't show here. The movie dares you to accept its premise at face value, and if you do, it rewards you with exactly what it promised: Hulk Hogan triumphing over a world that does not deserve him.

It is terrible. It is also perfectly on brand.

After *No Holds Barred* came a number of terrible movies that saw Hogan trying to volunteer for service in the burgeoning action star industrial complex. To some Hogan surely seemed like a natural fit, a Schwarzenegger without the halting accent. But the Hogan brand insisted on itself too much, and the self-awareness was shockingly nonexistent. *Mr. Nanny*, *Suburban Commando*, *Santa with Muscles*—

there's nothing I could tell you that the titles don't immediately convey, and the less said about them the better.

What interests me most is his magnum opus, the part to which he dedicated the most time outside of the ring: that of Hurricane Spencer in the TV series *Thunder in Paradise.*

If *No Holds Barred* is Hogan's attempt at cinematic dominance, *Thunder in Paradise* was his acceptance of his lot in life as more of a Hasselhoff than a Stallone. This is Hogan scaled down just enough to fit into a weekly action-adventure format, which somehow makes everything about him even more ridiculous.

Thunder in Paradise plays like someone fed *Baywatch*, *Knight Rider*, and professional wrestling into an algorithm that had recently suffered a concussion. Hogan plays a muscle-bound adventurer with a talking high-tech boat, because of course he does. The show is allergic to logic, physics, and budgetary restraint, but it understands something crucial: Hogan is not a dramatic actor, but he is a reliable presence.

This is where his acting career finds its most natural home. Television forgives repetition. It forgives limited range. It rewards familiarity. Hogan does not need to surprise you; he needs to show up, deliver a handful of lines, throw a punch, smile like he's in on a joke that no one else quite understands, and reset for next week.

His performance in *Thunder in Paradise* is not good, but it is comfortable. Hogan is relaxed in a way he never quite is in movies. He is no longer carrying the weight of the Hulkamania myth on his shoulders—this is 1994 after all, when the craze almost seemed to have died out. It feels like a retirement gig, and Hogan is just another syndicated action guy with a gimmick and a paycheck. The stakes are lower, and so is the strain. In a strange way, this is Hogan at his most honest as an actor. He is not trying to be something else. He is being Hulk Hogan in a context that has learned how to work around him.

* * *

In the end, it's fair to say that Hulk Hogan is a bad actor, a very bad actor, at least on the screen. Hogan does not disappear into roles. He does not transform. He does not modulate. He projects. He asserts. He overwhelms. These are not acting skills so much as survival traits developed in front of hostile crowds and under unforgiving lights. As his penchant for lying and his uncomfortable last act in the WWF tell us, the most difficult parts of Hogan's life stem from his inability to separate the man from the character, and if Hulk Hogan and Terry Bollea are the same person, then was he ever acting in the first place?

Regardless, it would be unfair to say Hogan failed at acting, because that assumes acting was ever the point. Hogan's film and television career is better understood as a case study in what happens when a persona is so large it bends every medium it enters. Movies did not change Hulk Hogan. Hulk Hogan changed movies, usually for the worse, occasionally for the weirdly memorable. He was always more of an event than an actor.

And this should not distract from the fact that pro wrestling is its own form of acting, and Hogan was one of the most significant craftsmen of the trade to ever live. Look at his most dramatic moments—*Piper's Pit* with André, or his tears when he was carrying Elizabeth in his arms—and it's not sacrilege to laugh. He was a pretty bad actor in the wrestling world, too, and nobody should ever hold that against him.

CHAPTER 10

THE RELAPSE

HULK HOGAN VS. WCW

Hulk Hogan didn't have a monumental goodbye in the WWF; he slowly faded away, like a tan line in winter. By the early 1990s, the man who had once been professional wrestling's sun had slowly drifted out of orbit. The cartoon boom was over. The prayers and vitamins had curdled into something faintly embarrassing. WrestleMania stopped being built around him, and for the first time since Reagan was in office, Hulk Hogan looked less like the future of wrestling than its most expensive piece of nostalgia. When his WWF run petered out, WCW was more than happy to pay that price.

On the June 11, 1994, episode of *WCW Monday Nitro*, we start off with a relatively empty segment from Disney MGM Studios in Orlando as they await the arrival of Hogan, who will be conducting his first press conference as a WCW employee. Finally, a few segments later, he arrives, sitting in the back of a red convertible while a hundred or so fans—and I use this term loosely, because this is a tourist destination and a chance to be on TV, so who knows if they're there on purpose—listlessly surround the car. Confetti rains from the skies as Gene Okerlund and Eric Bischoff on commentary vamp to fill space. Mean Gene earnestly calls it "unequivocally the greatest day that professional wrestling has ever seen."

Hogan had departed the WWF with a promise to Vince McMahon that he would never work for the competition—just one lie among many. WCW honcho Eric Bischoff had approached Hogan on the set of *Thunder in Paradise* and offered him another lease on stardom and a chance to prove his relevance to McMahon and the world, and Hogan said yes. He arrived in WCW with a theoretical bang, but the execution was the exhale of a whoopie cushion.

As if the arrival of the '80s icon and the notion of the parade itself didn't sufficiently date the proceedings, Gene goes on: "This is like a ticker tape parade like the Babe is coming to town, like Henry Aaron is celebrating." Nothing screams youth and vitality like the golden age of baseball.

When the press conference begins, Hogan seems legitimately excited, but an octave higher, thinner, more antic, and significantly more Ninja Turtle–infused than I had remembered him in the WWF, as if he had swapped in the PEDs for helium. He talks repeatedly about wanting to earn immortality by taking on Ric Flair—a good start, and a gesture at restitution for dodging him in the WWF—and then wanders into more philosophical territory. When asked a question about whether his move to WCW was like Joe Montana joining the Chiefs, Hogan said, "Well, you know something, brother, the big man upstairs, he moves mountains, dude, and in seven days and seven nights, he created the heavens and the earth. And on the eighth day, dude, he created Hulkamania."

Hogan's arrival in WCW in 1994 was framed in biblical terms because it was, in a sense, a resurrection. WCW rolled out the red-and-yellow carpet and then kept rolling until it wrapped around half of Disney World. Rather than place Hogan in a wrestling ring, they put on a parade—an actual, honest-to-God ticker-tape parade—complete with floats, balloons, and the vague civic delirium usually reserved for Super Bowl winners and cartoon mice. It was wrestling's most ambitious attempt to convince itself, and everyone watching, that it was finally the big leagues.

There's something about wrestling's relationship with sincerity that makes moments like this fascinating. Wrestling thrives on exaggeration, but only when that exaggeration is winking. Hogan's parade wasn't ironic; it was earnest. WCW truly believed that Hogan's mere presence would confer legitimacy, star power, and mainstream relevance. They treated him like a conquering hero returning from a victorious war, rather than a forty-year-old performer changing companies because the old arrangement had run out of road. Watching it now, the parade feels like someone throwing himself a birthday party and hoping his crush notices.

In a WCW that had for so long lagged behind the WWF in ratings and general pop cultural significance, Hogan, even in his diminished state, was treated as superior to all of WCW's established stars, because at its very base, pro wrestling is a contest of renown, of popularity—and because, no matter who you're signing, a wrestler is only as big as the promotion says he is.

WCW, in its latest attempt at reinvention—now with former announcer Bischoff as the leader—had been signing up WWF names at a fast clip. Macho Man was there, as was Okerlund. In the territorial era, stars went back and forth between promotions all the time; many of them worked multiple territories simultaneously. But since Vince took over the WWF, contracts had become more standardized, and pro wrestling "free agency" was starting to become a going concern. It was common in these years for WCW and the WWF to sign each other's wrestlers when their contracts were up; after all, they were the two biggest games in town, and there were only so many TV-ready wrestlers to offer money to. Flair and his Horsemen cohorts Tully Blanchard and Arn Anderson all did spells in the WWF, as did their rival Dusty Rhodes. But none of them lasted, and they all ended up back in WCW; the audiences for the two promotions were markedly different, and stardom in one place didn't necessarily mean success in the other.

It wasn't until Bischoff, though, that stars were poached by WCW specifically for the sake of siphoning fans from the WWF. That was Bischoff's goal and the objective signed off by corporate overlord Ted Turner. When Hulk Hogan became available, Bischoff and Turner backed up the Brinks truck.

Hogan arrived in WCW carrying two things: his name and his past. WCW wanted both, but they only really knew how to use one. They had Hogan wrestle Flair almost immediately, because that was the biggest match they could imagine—and the match that WWF had inexplicably avoided. It was a match that felt historic on paper and oddly weightless in execution, like two action figures finally sharing the same toy box years after you stopped playing with them.

Flair was an immaculate performer, and while he was a few years removed from his prime, he could still bring the house down with his reactive athleticism and the immediacy of his in-ring storytelling. (Flair, despite being past his prime, would wrestle for almost thirty more years before retiring in 2023.) Hogan wasn't far from his peak either, because he was never much of an in-ring standout, but age seemed to wear on him more obviously. Losing a half step shifted his routine from minimalist perfection to clunky self-reference. The comparison to Flair didn't help much either. Flair represented WCW's in-house legacy; Hogan represented the outside world's idea of wrestling superstardom. Putting them together should have been alchemy. Instead, it was a reminder that wrestling history doesn't automatically convert into wrestling chemistry.

This was the core problem of Hogan's early WCW run: Everything was built on the assumption that nostalgia could substitute for creativity. Hogan was positioned exactly as he had been in the WWF, minus the institutional muscle memory that made that positioning work. He was still the smiling hero, still cutting promos that sounded like they'd been written in 1987 and left folded up in a back pocket ever since. The crowds cheered because crowds cheer Hulk Hogan, but there was an audible lag to it—a sense that people were applauding out of obligation rather than excitement. WCW mistook recognition for engagement, which is an easy error to make when your biggest signing is also the most famous wrestler who ever lived.

The booking reflected this confusion. Hogan was the top guy

by default, not by momentum. He won titles because that's what Hulk Hogan does. He feuded with monsters because that's what Hulk Hogan does. He overcame odds that didn't feel especially dire because that's what Hulk Hogan does. The stories weren't bad so much as unnecessary. They existed to justify Hogan's presence, not to explore it.

There was also the tonal problem. WCW in the mid-1990s was a strange, overstuffed ecosystem. It had remnants of old-school Southern wrestling, flashes of modern athleticism, and a creeping wave of cartoon absurdity. Hogan didn't bridge these worlds; he floated above them, insulated by his own mythology. When he teamed with Randy Savage, it felt like a traveling nostalgia act. When he battled the Dungeon of Doom, it felt like a children's show that had lost track of its target audience.

The Dungeon of Doom deserves special mention, if only because it represents the nadir of Hogan's pre-nWo WCW tenure. This was wrestling villainy filtered through a Halloween store clearance rack and a fog machine. Faces appeared in shadows. Voices boomed ominously. Earthquake was there, dressed as a literal shark. Hogan reacted to all of this with the same wide-eyed intensity he'd once reserved for Cold War–era heels, selling nonsense as if it were an existential threat. (Kevin Sullivan, one of the bookers for the company and the on-screen leader of the Dungeon, told me that he invented the Dungeon to give all of Hogan's backstage friends something to do.) The Dungeon begat the Giant, a "seven-foot-tall" Paul Wight, who was initially billed as André the Giant's son. Everything was a throwback; the most novel thing they did in the Giant feud was have him and Hogan face off in monster trucks on a rooftop.

What made this period so damaging, in retrospect, is that it threatened to calcify Hogan's legacy. Without what came next, this could have been the final chapter: the aging superhero bouncing between companies, replaying his greatest hits for diminishing returns. WCW was embalming Hogan rather than reinventing him. Every title win added weight to his résumé but drained urgency from his character. Hogan became less a protagonist than a fixed point around which the rest of the promotion awkwardly orbited, just like in the WWF but with less inertia.

And yet, there were hints—tiny, almost accidental hints—that something wasn't working. Crowds started booing, not out of malice but out of boredom. Hogan's act, once revolutionary in its simplicity, had become predictable in its righteousness. The red and yellow felt forced rather than aspirational. WCW, perhaps without realizing it, had created the conditions for rebellion by both ignoring its own history and refusing to acknowledge that the world had changed.

Hogan himself seemed trapped by his own iconography. The man who had once embodied wrestling's ability to synthesize pop culture, masculinity, and spectacle was now a museum exhibit, complete with explanatory plaques. WCW treated him like a solution rather than a question, and in doing so, guaranteed creative stagnation.

That's the great irony of Hogan's early WCW years: They were both wildly indulgent and strangely cautious. The company gave him everything—money, spotlight, ceremonial parades—but didn't ask him to be anything other than what he already was. The result was a run that felt simultaneously dominant and hollow. Hogan was always winning, always central, and yet totally unnecessary.

Had the story ended there, Hogan's career would read very differently today. The image of him in WCW might be defined by smoke-filled lairs, overproduced feuds, and that parade—God, that parade—rolling past confused tourists who had no idea they were witnessing the symbolic peak of wrestling excess. It would be the story of a legend who mistook relevance for reverence and paid for it in creative entropy. Instead, this fallow period became the setup.

The brilliance of what followed lies partly in how starkly it contrasted with what came before. Hogan's WCW arrival promised transformation and delivered cold comfort. It was only after this long stretch of creative malaise that the real reinvention became possible. The audience had to tire of the old Hulk Hogan before it could accept a new one. WCW had to exhaust every nostalgic impulse before it could embrace something genuinely dangerous. Hulk Hogan mattered at this moment because he pulled back the curtain in a way he never had in the WWF, proving that creative bankruptcy could be its own starting point.

The pre-nWo Hogan era exists now as a necessary embarrassment—a reminder that legends don't fade gracefully by default, and that sometimes the most important chapters in wrestling history are the ones that almost ruin everything. It's the sound of an engine idling, a parade going in circles, a company celebrating the past because it doesn't yet know how to imagine the future.

In that sense, it's perfect. Wrestling has always been best when it accidentally tells the truth about itself.

CHAPTER 11

THE TURNCOAT

HULK HOGAN VS. HIMSELF

Professional wrestling is built on promises it can't keep. The biggest one—the one it sells to kids, advertisers, and occasionally itself—is that its heroes are immortal. That these athletes are gods, that the guy who taught you what right and wrong looked like will still be there when you come back years later, unchanged, muscles intact, morals preserved in amber. It's an odd point of tension in pro wrestling; a lot of pro wrestling's historical antecedents—theater, mythology, fables—are timeless in a way that its most straightforward precursor (legitimate wrestling, or boxing, or real sport in general) is absolutely not.

The issue is complicated by the fact that so many stars do seem to wrestle forever, and even the ones who don't, exist in our memories (and video collections) like our favorite superheroes, as ageless, symbolic golems. Any given wrestling broadcast will lean on both halves unthinkingly: that wrestlers are putting their bodies on the line at every moment, and that heroes last forever. Hulk Hogan himself, who looked relatively the same at his death as he did in 1983, was called "The Immortal One" right up until his last day, even as he was said to be in mortal danger in feud after feud.

Sometimes that false premise ends in tragedy. Sometimes it ends in a bit of creative genius. Wrestling needs that promise to exist, but it also needs to violate it periodically just to prove it's alive. On July 7, 1996, at Bash at the Beach, wrestling broke that promise in public. Loudly. And once it did, there was no going back.

Hogan joining the nWo will be remembered as a heel turn. But it was more than that: a referendum—on nostalgia, on aging stars, on whether wrestling could admit that its audience had changed. Hogan didn't betray the fans that night—he confronted them with a version of himself they already suspected was real.

The formation of the New World Order was shocking because the hero turned villain. It was *more* shocking because the villain sounded right.

* * *

To fully grasp why Hogan's heel turn mattered, consider how long the lie had been wobbling. By the mid-1990s, Hulk Hogan was still wrestling's eternal center, but at this point it was little more than a courtesy. Hogan was still famous, still physically imposing in a way that bent reality, but the culture that once needed him had moved on. Wrestling fans had changed, and wrestling had not.

The babyface ideals Hogan represented—clear morals, unambiguous triumph, performative patriotism—might have been meaningful in the 1980s, but they felt increasingly out of step with a post–Cold War, pre-internet America. Movies were darker. Television heroes were sarcastic and self-aware. Even sports had shifted toward personalities over institutions. Hulkamania wasn't offensive; it was inert. It existed, but it no longer moved people.

Meanwhile, WCW was a company in search of relevance rather than stability. It had money, a national platform, and a roster full of talent, but it lacked the one thing wrestling needs most: urgency, the kind of creative electricity that, as they say in the business, puts butts in seats. The bare-knuckle vitality of the '80s days of Crockett territorial programming was gone, and what was left in the national television era felt oddly small. The audience could sense that disconnect. They weren't rejecting wrestling; they were rejecting monotony.

Then Scott Hall walked in through the crowd.

From the moment Scott Hall—known to that point as the WWF's Razor Ramon—appeared on WCW television in May 1996, he felt like an immaculate programming error, a mistake that had wandered onto the wrong show. He was not in tights or ring gear; he looked like someone who wasn't supposed to be there at all. No music. No introduction. Just jeans, a toothpick, and the implication of a hole in the space-time continuum. Most fans assumed he was still a WWF employee, and his appearance here did nothing to contradict that. He climbed into the ring, interrupting a match, and uttered the coolest, most disruptive phrase in wrestling at the time: "You know who I am, but you don't know why I'm here."

Kevin Nash—"Diesel" in the WWF—followed soon after, bringing with him scale, menace, and credibility. Together, they weren't framed as new signings (although they were—the latest Bischoff acquisitions from the competition) so much as intruders. The brilliance of the Outsiders, as they were called, was that they exploited the one thing wrestling almost never lets itself exploit: the doubt that comes with an unreliable narrator.

Were they representing another company? Was this a storyline or a lawsuit waiting to happen? WCW didn't answer those questions at first because answering them would have ruined the effect. The angle lived in the gray area between fiction and speculation, and that gray area felt thrilling because it mirrored how fans actually experienced wrestling. Everyone knew the results were predetermined, but every well-thrown punch instinctively brings that into question. Now, nobody knew how much of what they were seeing was supposed to be happening.

Hall and Nash didn't need to cheat to feel dangerous. Their threat was existential. They weren't trying to win titles; they were trying to hijack the narrative. Wrestling villains traditionally want power, but the Outsiders wanted control of the conversation. That distinction mattered.

From the beginning, the Outsiders angle demanded a third man. Not just for balance but for legitimacy. Two invaders can be repelled. Three suggest infrastructure. A system. A future. Speculation ran wild. The third man was supposed to be a surprise, but it also had to be someone who could explain everything retroactively. Someone whose presence reframed the entire angle, not just advanced it. It had to be someone whose very existence raised the stakes.

In the end, according to Bischoff and the parties involved, it was either going to be Hulk Hogan or the babyface standard-bearer of WCW before Hogan's arrival, Sting. Sting would have been interesting, but the inevitable next step—seeing this new faction endlessly feud with Hogan—would not. To fulfill the promise of the Outsiders angle, the only answer was the one person nobody could bring themselves to suspect. The third man had to be Hulk Hogan.

At Bash at the Beach 1996, WCW stalwarts Sting, Lex Luger, and "Macho Man" Randy Savage (it's a stretch to call Savage a stalwart, sure, but he was famous enough for the role) are set to face off against the interloper team of Hall, Nash, and a mystery partner, with the soul of WCW on the line. No third man materializes, so the match is three against two. The Outsiders avail themselves well, considering, but the heroes keep a slight upper hand when, during a melee, Nash deliberately hits Savage with an illegal low blow. The ref doesn't see it, so out marches Hulk Hogan to defend WCW and the rule-abiding order of wrestling. Or so it seems.

The announce team included Bobby "The Brain" Heenan, a longtime foe of Hogan in the WWF who continued their beef through his arch commentary in WCW. The announcers were legitimately not privy to what was about to happen—management preferred to keep them in the dark and let them react organically. Falling back on his anti-Hulkamania shtick, Heenan accidentally presaged what was about to happen with what was meant to be a sarcastic question: "Whose side is he on?!"

Surprising everyone except those who took Heenan's query seriously, Hogan leg-drops Savage, tosses the referee out of the ring, and joins the Outsiders. Trash rains down from the crowd. For fans of my generation (and all following ones), this is the first time we had seen Hogan work heel; we may have favored other wrestlers over him, even his opponents, and he had not always availed himself as a moral icon, but he had always been presented that way. He had always been exactly the same character. Now he had turned our assumptions about him on their head. On the mic, he lays into the fans and explained his thought process:

"These two men right here came from a great big organization up north. And everybody was wondering who the third man was. Well, who knows more about that organization than me, brother? Well, let me tell you something! I made that organization a monster! I made people rich up there. I made the people that run that organization rich up there, brother. When it all came to pass, the name Hulk Hogan, the man Hulk Hogan, got bigger than the whole organization, brother!

"As far as I'm concerned, all this crap in the ring represents the fans out here. For two years, brother, for two years, I held my head high . . . I did everything for the charities . . . I did everything for the kids . . . and the reception I got when I came out here . . . you fans can stick it, brother, because if it wasn't for Hulk Hogan, you people wouldn't be here. If it wasn't for Hulk Hogan, Eric Bischoff would be still selling meat from a truck in Minneapolis, and if it wasn't for Hulk Hogan, all these Johnny-come-latelies that you see out here wrestling wouldn't be here. I was selling out the world, brother, while they were bumming gas to put in the car to get to high school."

This is the part people forget when they talk about the shock of the turn: Hogan made more sense than anyone else. He was the only choice that completed the argument the angle was making. But, more important than that, everything he said was true, or at least true in Terry Bollea's mind. For the first time, Hogan was leveling with the audience.

Hogan represented wrestling's old power structure. He was the establishment that Hall and Nash were supposedly rebelling against. By joining them, Hogan didn't just turn heel—he exposed the contradiction at the heart of that rebellion. The rebellion was the establishment. The future of wrestling was being dictated by the same people who had always dictated it, only now they were willing to admit it.

When Hogan came down the aisle at Bash at the Beach, the crowd still reacted on instinct. Cheers, relief, release. Hogan was here to save WCW from the invaders. That was the reflex. Then he dropped the leg.

Hogan's post-turn promo is often remembered for the phrase "New World Order" (actually, he first called it the "New World Organization," an uncharacteristic flub that let slip his anxiety in that epochal moment), but its real power came from its tone. It wasn't cool. It wasn't controlled. It wasn't even especially articulate. It sounded defensive, resentful, and raw.

Hogan didn't explain his betrayal in storyline terms. He didn't claim moral superiority or hidden virtue. He complained. He scolded. He accused the fans of turning on him first. It was the speech of a man who believed, sincerely, that he had earned eternal loyalty and was furious to learn that fandom expires.

In another era, that could have killed the angle. Wrestling villains aren't supposed to sound wounded. But in 1996, wounded confidence felt real. It matched the audience's own cynicism. The fans booed because Hogan was telling a truth they didn't want to hear.

The New World Order wasn't introduced as a cabal of supervillains. It was introduced as a grievance. A shared resentment between performers who believed they'd been undervalued, misunderstood, or prematurely dismissed. Hogan didn't turn evil—he turned honest.

Perhaps the most obvious—and enduring—question that spilled out of the Hogan turn: Why had McMahon never tried this in the WWF? The most obvious answer is that McMahon didn't think it would work. Later in life, Hogan insisted that he had pitched Vince a heel turn at various points over his WWF career. It's generally hard to believe Hogan on such matters, but at the same time it's hard to imagine it didn't cross his mind, since the turn is such an integral part of pro wrestling mythos. And after all, McMahon had turned André heel to get Hogan over. Why not turn Hogan to help the next generation? The most feasible answer to the question, though, is likely that McMahon didn't want to. Both he and Hogan were creatures of habit. And by the time it was a good idea, McMahon was ready to move on.

The immediate effects of the nWo were obvious and measurable. WCW's ratings surged. Merchandise exploded. Their black-and-white T-shirts became cultural artifacts. Wrestling felt current in a way it hadn't in years. Hogan undoubtedly extended the long tail of his cultural relevance by a decade or two. But the deeper impact was structural.

Before the nWo, wrestling storytelling, especially when it came to Hulkamania, was primarily episodic. Conflicts began, escalated, and resolved in neat arcs. Even long feuds were ultimately contained. The nWo rejected containment. It didn't want to just win a match; it wanted to linger. Its victories didn't feel like endings. Its defeats didn't feel final. The matches themselves sat in the shadow of the revolutionary spirit.

All of this changed how fans watched wrestling. Attention became a currency. Continuity mattered. You were rewarded for remembering who had betrayed whom, who wore which colors, who hesitated for half a second too long during a run-in. Wrestling became more about the story you were tracking than the matches themselves.

The nWo also blurred the moral landscape. Babyfaces weren't automatically virtuous; they were reactionary. Heels weren't just rule-breakers; they were provocateurs. The question wasn't "Who's right?" but "Who's winning control?" That shift influenced everything that followed, across companies and eras. Wrestling learned that ambiguity—the very thing that Hulk Hogan had battled against for his entire career up to that point—wasn't a weakness. Ambiguity was the hook.

* * *

For Hogan personally, the nWo wasn't just a reinvention. It was a recalibration of his entire legacy. "Hollywood" Hogan was not simply the inverse of Hulkamania—it was a commentary on it. He had a dense black stubble connecting his blond sideburns and mustache, sunglasses obscuring his baby blue eyes, and a slow, arrogant strut. These things seemed to mock the past as much as replace it. Hogan turned his famous flexes and poses into taunts. He weaponized his own iconography.

This allowed Hogan—finally—to age in public without pretending he wasn't aging. He could be slower, lazier, more self-indulgent, and it all fit the character. The crowd didn't demand moral clarity from him anymore. They demanded realism, or at least something that felt like it.

The cost of this transformation was permanence. Once Hogan acknowledged the transactional nature of his relationship with the audience, he couldn't fully unacknowledge it. Every subsequent babyface run carried an implicit wink. Every patriotic speech felt conditional. But that permanence is what made the turn meaningful. Hogan accepted that his myth had cracks and chose to live through them rather than pretend they weren't there.

Though the nWo revolutionized heeldom and led to the breakouts of several new stars like Goldberg, the Hogan nWo years weren't entirely free of uncomfortable nostalgia. With him now ensconced as a heel, WCW brought in old (largely out of work) Hogan foes like Roddy Piper and the Ultimate Warrior to try to recapture their WWF-era glory. Needless to say, these did not come across as innovation. The nWo breathed new life into the sport, but the fallout was almost immediate: Hogan, reinvigorated by his villainy's success and by the return of his centrality, became a backstage politician to a degree previously unfathomed, as if his on-screen heroism had been keeping his real-life baser instincts at bay.

The lowest moment (or second lowest after the Fingerpoke of Doom, more on that later) was the match between Hogan and Sting at Starrcade 1997. Sting—formerly a neon-colored babyface—had grown dark and despondent in the nWo era. He loomed in the rafters, a constant vague threat to Hogan and his partners. When they finally met in the ring for the WCW title, the anticipation was high—but the execution was terrible. The plan for the ending of the match was fine, if a little too cute: Hogan would pin Sting, and the referee—paid off by Hogan (in an evocation of the Hogan-André Main Event match)—was to count to three in hyperspeed, illegally awarding Hogan the win. Then, new WCW hire Bret Hart would come out and demand the match be restarted (a reference to his own departure from the WWF in the infamous Montreal Screwjob), after which Sting would win the title. The only problem was that the referee didn't count quickly. Hogan won with a totally normal one-two-three, and so he deserved to win the match, making Hart look like a fool for complaining, and Sting like a dupe for celebrating his eventual win. There has been much debate over the years about whether the referee just messed up, or whether Hulk had convinced him to do it to make Hogan look good. When we have reached the point that the most compelling (and disappointing) part of any Hogan story is litigating the part we don't see on the screen, we've discovered rock bottom.

The kind reading of the situation from a macro view is that the New World Order eventually became too successful for its own good. As the stable expanded, it lost the intimacy that made it compelling. The original grievance gave way to bureaucracy. What began as a hostile takeover became a corporate sprawl. That overreach is often cited as evidence that the nWo "went too far," but that misunderstands the nature of the angle. Revolutions don't end because they succeed too much; they end because they become systems. The nWo stopped feeling dangerous once it felt inevitable.

Even in decline, though, its influence remained. Wrestling never went back to the pre-nWo world. Reality-adjacent storytelling became expected. Audiences became more comfortable booing their childhood heroes and cheering their former villains. They were in on the big lie now, and there was no returning to the status quo.

But the impermanence of Hogan and the nWo, or its success relative to its potential, shouldn't have a bearing on the importance of Hogan's heel turn. By turning heel, by embracing the uncertainty and thumbing his nose at the fans for the first time in years, Hogan realized that the only immortality in pro wrestling comes with adaptability. It comes with fluidity. It comes with taking your biggest weakness and making it your biggest strength. Pro wrestling provides a platform for that—you just have to get a little trash thrown at you sometimes.

Hogan joining the nWo endures not because it was surprising but because it was necessary. Wrestling had reached a point where pretending the past could carry the future was doing more harm than good. The turn didn't destroy Hulkamania; it contextualized it. Hulk Hogan matters because he forced pro wrestling to admit that its audience had grown up—and that growing up didn't mean abandoning the past, just interrogating it. Hogan didn't ask for forgiveness. He demanded acknowledgment. The crowd responded with rejection—which, in wrestling, is all the acknowledgment anyone could ask for. Boos are as good as cheers; any reaction, any investment by the crowd is the goal. Wrestling got better for Hogan's embrace of rejection.

In the end, the red and yellow didn't die that night at Bash at the Beach. It became history instead of policy. And that distinction—between honoring the past and being ruled by it—is the line wrestling crossed when Hogan dropped that leg. Everything after has been wrestling trying, in one way or another, to live on the other side of that line.

CHAPTER 12

THE OPERATOR

HULK HOGAN VS. POLITICS

After turning heel, Hogan seemed to regain all of the power of his '80s heyday, and even though his presence was at times overbearing and tiresome, he was undeniable. Hogan didn't just loom over professional wrestling in the late 1990s; he was the weather system. And the storm of the century was the so-called Fingerpoke of Doom on January 4, 1999. Wrestling, in that moment, was humid with success and ripe for rot. The business was making money, drawing ratings, and devouring itself in real time. And Hogan—ever the symbol of wrestling's appetites—was both symptom and cause.

How could a single extended index finger feel like an extinction-level event? It all has to do with Hogan. The glory of Hogan's heel turn was relatively brief, and soon he rediscovered the exhausting inevitability of his late-WWF days, only this time he was a villain, so the fans could boo him openly for it. He was walking a fine line—there are few sources of real villainy in modern pro wrestling, since fans will cheer a compelling heel, but leaning into things the fans actually dislike for the sake of boos risks turning the audience off entirely. It was the era of the internet, and rumors of Hogan's backstage power plays became constant fodder for plugged-in fans. It's a fact that he had absolute creative control written into his contract, and though he had seemed to manage fine over the years with mere de facto creative control, he had been popular enough for the fans to forgive it.

The strictures of his contract with WCW—including the enormous amount of money he was making—made him feel like an onus. That's not to say his existence was burdensome—he might have been the most effective heel ever in his nWo peak, and channeled correctly he could have continued that way for another decade. The problem was that he was a burden to creativity. He was a walking contract clause. A guaranteed reaction that had warped into surefire groan. Hogan had remade himself, turning from patriotic demigod to black-bearded heel messiah. That heel turn didn't just revive his career; it jump-started a boom. WCW rode it to the top of the ratings, beat Vince McMahon's WWF in television ratings for eighty-three straight weeks, and convinced itself that momentum was a strategy.

But momentum as a strategy becomes monotony without much effort. Nothing new and exciting was going to happen with Hogan around. Well, nothing good, anyway.

The Fingerpoke of Doom—and yes, this is the accepted name for the event, despite its never being named as such on WCW television—was the peak of Hogan's perceived egocentrism. It has a Wikipedia page and everything, something most major wrestling *matches* don't have. The booking in WCW was antic and overly convoluted, though the logic behind it made sense at the time. During the Monday Night Wars, the five-year ratings battle between WCW and the WWF on Monday-night television, keeping eyes on the screen required constant surprises. But when those surprises fly in the face of continuity, character development, and audience satisfaction, it's harder to defend.

So bear with me as I attempt to relive the story on the eve of the Fingerpoke. Kevin Nash, Hogan's onetime partner, had split off from the nWo nine months prior, leading a babyface splinter cell called nWo Wolfpack; the remaining nWo, led by Hogan, became known as nWo Hollywood. Goldberg—the hulking babyface who was one of the only true new stars WCW made during the Monday Night Wars—was scheduled to face Nash for the WCW title, but Nash, through duplicitous means, got Goldberg arrested, and so the match was changed to Nash versus Hogan, who had just returned from a monthlong "retirement."

As the match begins and the two competitors stare each other down, announcer Tony Schiavone yells, "This is what pro wrestling—what World Championship Wrestling—is all about!" Perhaps we should have known something was up when we saw that Hogan couldn't be bothered to put on tights or take off his shirt; he stood there in a black tee and black baggy jeans, the most "dad trying to look cool" outfit possible. There was something unnerving about Hogan in this period, and the sartorial choices were evidence of it. The original nWo look—black T-shirt, jeans, and sunglasses—felt like a modern antihero's uniform, but the more he strayed from that, the more you got the feeling you were seeing the real Hogan, and it wasn't appealing. His character had gone from defiantly churlish to something approaching smarmy, and the ego seemed to leak from his real core as well.

Nash and Scott Hall, who had an effortless cool, could laugh and high-five and seem vital. As time wore on, Hogan seemed sort of like a creep. Their split made some sense in that regard, but it would be short-lived.

As the two enemies circle each other in the ring, Nash shoves Hogan into the corner, and then . . . Hogan pokes Nash in the chest with one finger. Nash collapses as if he had been hit by a truck. Hogan pins him and wins the title, and the two men celebrate together in the ring, a slapstick conspiracy well executed.

They celebrate alongside Scott Steiner, who had led nWo Hollywood in Hogan's absence, and who accompanied Hogan to the ring, and Scott Hall, who accompanied Nash, but who, until that match, had been aligned with the Hollywood faction. The nWo was reunited and up to its old tricks.

Goldberg makes it back from the jailhouse just in time to run in and beat up the heels. He is joined by fellow babyface Lex Luger, who . . . attacks Goldberg, joining the nWo. There's an old comedy saying about putting a hat on a hat that probably applies here. Three heel turns in one segment is approximately two too many.

It's hard to overstate how nakedly transactional the whole thing felt. The shock of the finish was outweighed by the insistence upon the superstar of yore. Even Nash, himself notorious for backstage politicking, lost out to the Hogan machine. The Fingerpoke of Doom told the audience that the past would always outrank the present, that star power meant seniority, and that the promotion's hottest new attraction—Goldberg—existed only to help Hogan's ratings. Wrestling had always been a business of illusions, but here the illusion was that there was no illusion. You could see the wires. You could feel the contract language. The story they were trying to tell was too close to reality, and fans weren't having it.

The most compelling question, really, is *why?* What was this meant to accomplish that a more straightforward sequence of events wouldn't have done equally well? Much of the speculation, of course, has to do with Hogan's creative control. In the preceding months, Hogan had lost the WCW title to Goldberg, culminating an epic storyline that fans—and logic—had demanded. It was truly a thing of beauty. But what the fans demanded was not just a title change—it was a change of direction. Following Goldberg's big win, the next WCW pay-per-view was headlined by . . . Hulk Hogan, teaming up with Dennis Rodman against Diamond Dallas Page and Karl Malone. (Yes, that's an NBA player on each team, for no particularly urgent reason.) The PPV after that? Hogan headlined again, this time teaming with nWo mouthpiece Bischoff against Page and Jay Leno (Yes, talk show host Jay Leno.) After that? Goldberg wasn't even on the card, and didn't show up, while Hogan was part of a nine-person main event. Okay, okay—what about the one after that? Goldberg finally got the main event spot, facing DDP for the title. It was a truly great match. The only problem was that the event ran long, so the pay-per-view feed ended for most viewers before they got to see it, leaving them with the lasting impression of the preceding match, Hogan versus the Warrior (the "Ultimate" part was owned by the WWF), a rematch of their WrestleMania VII showdown. According to anyone except Hogan and Bischoff (the guy signing the checks), the match only existed to stroke Hogan's ego, to let him get his win back from Warrior. (If you're keeping score, yes, Hogan was more concerned about his win-loss record in a staged sport than in telling a good story.) It is widely decried as the worst WCW match ever. Hogan took responsibility, because he tried to throw a fireball in Warrior's face and ended up setting his own mustache on fire, but that really lets the other fourteen minutes of this truly deplorable match (and its truly inane build) off the hook. If only Hogan had been able to set fire to the whole thing.

Why a fingerpoke in particular? It's likely that Nash's sway played a part in this mess; the match was booked in such a way as to make both men look strong. The fact that the finished product was insultingly bad was secondary to the protection of the two egos at play. There's an argument that this angle effectively acknowledged that the storytelling in WCW had spun out of control, that putting the belt back on Hogan and reuniting the nWo was a hard reset that could take WCW back to its Bash at the Beach glory, but if the pathway there is doubling down on the problems that got you here, it's hard to believe there's any real contrition.

Which is all to say that Hogan's backstage sway—both through his contract and through his tight relationship with Bischoff—or at least the specter of it, became the legitimate target of blame for most WCW problems. The way every Hogan opponent from WrestleMania III on had been treated, culminating in WCW foes Sting and Goldberg, made it clear by this point that Hogan's main concern was hogging the spotlight. It's a dire commentary on Hogan as a person, but even more so in the world of pro wrestling, when the only way to real success is making your rivals look good.

The Fingerpoke of Doom probably gets too much credit. At another moment in time it might be remembered as a good, self-referential surprise. And getting the nWo back together to take on Goldberg could have made for months of good programming. But it lingers because it was a metaphor for all of the real problems dogging the company. WCW had money, stars, and cultural momentum, but it didn't have faith—in its future or in its audience's intelligence. It relied on proven names because proven names came with proven leverage. Hogan, who had once been synonymous with pro wrestling itself, became synonymous with his creative control clause. If wrestling is a morality play about power, then WCW wrote itself as the villain and dared you to boo.

* * *

The irony, of course, is that the Fingerpoke worked—just not in the way WCW hoped. That same night, millions of viewers flipped the channel to see Mick Foley win the WWF Championship. To make matters worse, they flipped over to watch it in part because Schiavone had told viewers that WWF was going to have the title change to try and spoil the results. (WWF shows were pretaped every other week, so WCW got the results and read them on-air to make the WWF seem like a second-rate company.) The crowd reaction for the Foley win was joyful and unscripted. It felt like something happening *for* the fans, not *to* them. Wrestling history loves its fork-in-the-road moments, and January 4, 1999, is one of the cleanest. One show chose consolidation; the other chose catharsis.

Hogan has always been at his most poignant when he embodies wrestling's contradictions. He is sincerity weaponized and cynicism disguised as professionalism. The Fingerpoke was latter-day Hulkamania distilled: Protect the brand, protect the brothers, protect the top. If that means deflating the narrative balloon you just spent a year inflating, so be it. Wrestling, after all, is about moments—and this moment belonged to him.

But wrestling is also about memory. Fans don't just remember what happened; they remember how it made them feel. The Fingerpoke didn't feel clever or daring. It felt lazy and exclusionary, like being reminded that the party was invitation-only and you were lucky to be watching through the window. WCW's audience had been trained to expect chaos, but this felt more like inanity—and worse, unnecessary monotony.

In hindsight, the Fingerpoke of Doom explains why WCW collapsed so quickly after peaking so high. The company mistook control for stability and nostalgia for loyalty. It treated the fans like marks again, like the old-fashioned dupes who weren't in on the sham of the business. That is unforgivable in the modern era. It forgot that wrestling booms are powered by the promise of next, not the comfort of *again*. When the business is hot, every decision feels survivable. When it cools, those same decisions become cautionary tales.

For the future of pro wrestling, the legacy is double-edged. On one side, the Fingerpoke became shorthand for everything fans fear: insider politics, creative stagnation, stars protecting spots at the expense of stories. It's invoked whenever a promotion seems to circle the wagons instead of building new ones. On the other side, it taught an entire generation of bookers and fans what not to do. Hulk Hogan matters because he taught us what the wrestling business *shouldn't* look like. Modern wrestling's obsession with long-term storytelling, clean finishes, and elevating new talent is, in part, a reaction to that single, anticlimactic poke.

It's fitting that the most remembered finger in the history of pro wrestling belongs to Hulk Hogan. He never had much of a move set anyway. Every simple thing he did was a hundred times more significant because it was him doing it. Even so, he couldn't have imagined that one simple poke would have lived on in such infamy.

Hogan's shadow still stretches across the industry. But the Fingerpoke of Doom froze that shadow in a particular shape. It showed what happens when wrestling forgets that its magic is borrowed and its audience is the lender.

CHAPTER 13

THE PRODIGAL SON

HULK HOGAN VS. LEGACY

When Hulk Hogan came home in 2002, the town had a new name—the company formally changed its name from the WWF to WWE in 2001 after a yearslong dispute with the World Wildlife Fund—but it was still a town he helped build. He was returning to a past that professional wrestling itself hadn't yet finished arguing with. The moment carried the strange emotional weight that only pro wrestling can generate: part homecoming, part victory lap, part historical reckoning.

Hogan's comeback came after WWE's 2001 purchase of WCW, the deal that officially ended the Monday Night Wars and unofficially froze an entire era of American pop culture in amber. Hogan reentered the story as both a character and a living artifact, a man whose career had helped fracture wrestling into rival mythologies and whose presence now forced those mythologies to reconcile.

When Hogan jumped to WCW in 1994, it was framed as a coup, a seismic shift that suggested wrestling might finally behave like a real entertainment industry, with stars who could cross company lines and bring audiences with them. Hogan jump-started the Monday Night Wars and signaled that Vince McMahon's monopoly on American wrestling superstardom was vulnerable. Hogan was the first real proof that the empire could bleed.

That bleeding became a hemorrhage in 1996, when Hogan turned heel and revealed himself as the third man in the New World Order. The nWo reinvented Hogan and reinvented the grammar of wrestling. It collapsed the boundary between character and reality and turned the audience's growing cynicism into fuel. Hogan, once the avatar of Reagan-era optimism, became the embodiment of late-'90s cultural exhaustion: sneering, self-aware, and cool in a way that felt both forced and accidental. WCW surged, Nitro beat Raw, and for the first time Vince McMahon found himself reacting rather than dictating.

And yet, for all the revolutionary energy Hogan helped unleash, the Monday Night Wars ended not with a dramatic final battle but with a slow erosion of trust, creativity, and institutional coherence. Vince McMahon didn't end the war by winning a single ratings week or simply outbooking WCW. He ended it by surviving. WWE adapted. It streamlined. It consolidated power. While WCW was collapsing under the weight of its own excess—too many contracts, too many promises, too little long-term planning—Time Warner, WCW's parent company, was sold, and WCW was determined to be expendable. WWE swooped in and bought their competition for pennies on the dollar, positioning itself as the last standing "major league" American wrestling promotion. In storyline, Vince was set to announce the acquisition of WCW when his son Shane swooped in and bought it instead. The war didn't end with fireworks; it ended with paperwork.

That context is crucial, because Hogan's WWE return in 2002 only made sense in a world where WWE had already won. Hogan didn't come back as a conqueror or a rival. He came back as history reclaimed. WWE didn't need Hogan to compete anymore so much as it needed him to complete the story. By absorbing WCW and reintroducing its most famous defector, WWE could frame the entire Monday Night Wars as a detour—an exciting one, sure, but ultimately temporary. Hogan's presence retroactively reinforced WWE's claim to be wrestling's central narrative, the place where all roads eventually lead back.

Initially, Hogan returned as "Hollywood" Hogan, complete with nWo branding. The nWo's WWE run overall was underwhelming—the group felt smaller in a WWE ring, its rebellious energy dulled by the very institution it once opposed. In WCW, the nWo felt like a hostile takeover, but in WWE, it felt like a reunion tour, an acknowledgment of past danger rather than a present threat. WWE was too self-aware, too dominant, to truly let the nWo destabilize it. (Also, in storyline, Vince was the one who hired the nWo.)

But the failure of the nWo angle in WWE wasn't just about

booking. It was about context. By 2002, wrestling audiences had changed. The Attitude Era had burned hot and fast, producing its own icons—Steve Austin, The Rock, Goldberg—who weren't just stars but cultural moments. Hogan, even as Hollywood Hogan, now represented something older. His rebellion had been absorbed into the mainstream. His antiestablishment energy now read as legacy branding.

And then, almost by accident, everything clicked.

The turning point came at WrestleMania X8, in a match that was supposed to be symbolic but became something much larger: Hogan versus The Rock, one of the biggest stars of the modern era. (A star so big that he was launching his own Hollywood career, one that would overshadow Hogan's to the point that it actually changed Hogan's own legacy.) On paper, it was another passing-of-the-torch story, the aging icon facing the modern megastar. In execution, it became one of the most emotionally complex matches in pro wrestling history.

From the opening moments, the 68,000-person Toronto crowd rejected the script. Hogan, the villain, was cheered. The Rock, the hero, was met with a more divided reaction. What followed was not a traditional match but a negotiation between eras, mediated by the audience. Hogan worked like it was 1987. He posed. He soaked in the crowd. He slowed the pace to a crawl. And the crowd went with him—not ironically but sincerely; not even nostalgically, because time itself seemed to rewind. For one night, Hulk Hogan wasn't a relic or a heel or a punchline. He was the thing itself.

The significance of that match goes beyond its star power or crowd reaction. Hogan vs. Rock functioned as wrestling's collective memory made physical. It wasn't about who should win; it was about what each man represented. The Rock was WWE's present and future, a performer shaped entirely within McMahon's system. Hogan was wrestling's past—not just WWE's but the industry's as a whole. When Hogan hulks up, it's a ritual, a shared language between performer and audience. At WrestleMania X8, that language still worked.

As the crowd vocally embraced Hogan, the two wrestlers in the ring adjusted on the fly, turning Hogan babyface mid-match and embracing the reaction rather than fighting it. In doing so, the company demonstrated the lesson it had learned during—and after—the Monday Night Wars: Control the frame, but listen to the crowd. Hogan's subsequent WWE title win later that year felt almost superficial in comparison. The real victory had already happened. Hogan had been reabsorbed into WWE—not as a threat but as a foundational myth.

In terms of Hogan's relationship with WWE, the return was a reconciliation without an apology. WWE didn't need Hogan to repent for WCW, and Hogan didn't need WWE to validate his legacy. Instead, both sides benefited from a kind of historical ceasefire. By absorbing WCW, WWE got to claim Hogan's entire career—early Hulkamania, the nWo years, and the final nostalgia run—as part of its narrative. Hogan got to end his full-time career where it began, positioned once again as wrestling's ultimate star rather than its most famous defector.

In the broader scope of wrestling history, Hogan's return symbolized the end of wrestling's last true civil war. After 2002, there would be competition, alternatives, even revolutions of scale—but never again a moment when the industry felt split down the middle, with two corporations fighting for cultural dominance. Hogan had been the face of peak WWF and the face of the split. His return closed the loop.

There's a temptation to see Hogan's WWE comeback as purely sentimental, a victory lap for a star and a company eager to canonize itself. But that undersells its importance. Hulk Hogan matters because he allowed pro wrestling to acknowledge its own contradictions: that rebellion eventually becomes tradition, that stars outgrow companies and then get folded back into them, that history in wrestling is never erased—only rewritten, rebranded, and reintroduced.

Hulk Hogan didn't just come back to WWE in 2002. He came back to remind wrestling what it had been, what it had survived, and how much of its identity was still tied to a man tearing his shirt in half while a crowd decided, one last time, to believe.

CHAPTER 14

THE FOUNDER

HULK HOGAN VS. VINCE MCMAHON

There's a moment in the spring of 2003 when Hulk Hogan—arguably the most recognizable figure professional wrestling ever produced—stood in a WWE ring and denied being himself. He did it under oath. He did it while wearing a red, white, and blue mask. He did it while Vince McMahon, the man who made him Hulk Hogan in the first place, glared from a few feet away, veins bulging with a fury that felt both theatrical and disturbingly sincere.

This was the Mr. America storyline, and it was ridiculous. It was also, in a strange and very wrestling way, honest.

Hogan's 2002 return to WWE had already been a victory lap disguised as a comeback. WrestleMania X8, Hogan vs. The Rock, had settled—at least emotionally—the question of whether the Hulkster still mattered. The Toronto crowd told us everything: Hogan mattered, maybe more than ever. The yellow-and-red past outshone the future, and Hogan, the eternal opportunist, slid back into the role of heroic icon as if the last six years hadn't happened.

But nostalgia only lasts so long. WWE in 2003 didn't really need Hulk Hogan the competitor. What it needed was Hulk Hogan the idea. And a battle of ideas in the world of pro wrestling always ends up in a brawl. So Hogan didn't feud with another wrestler. He feuded with Vince McMahon himself.

On paper, this made perfect sense. McMahon had already positioned himself as the ultimate villain of WWE, the living embodiment of corporate cruelty, ego, and control. Hogan, meanwhile, was wrestling's most famous icon of excess and self-mythology. Their real-life history was tangled, messy, and combustible: lawsuits, betrayals, rival promotions, whispered accusations about money and credit and ego. If WWE was going to do "meta" storytelling—and by 2003, that was practically its house style—this was the richest vein left to mine. What's striking, looking back, is how naked the whole thing felt.

It started on March 23, 2003, at No Way Out, when Hogan had a rematch against The Rock. Vince McMahon comes to ringside and distracts the referee, allowing The Rock to get a chair and club Hogan with it. The Rock wins, and McMahon takes a victory lap the next night on *Raw*, proclaiming the end of Hulkamania. He announced a new era: McMahonamania. Hogan takes issue with this, naturally—Hulkamania was not Vince's to squash. Vince lays into Hogan, saying he hated him; "hate" is a word used unusually rarely in pro wrestling, despite the emotions involved, and coming from McMahon's mouth it had the ring of truth. He hated Hogan for testifying against him in the steroid trial, he hated him for going to WCW. The feud played out like couples therapy conducted at shouting volume. On an episode of *Smackdown*, the two put everything on the table.

Hogan: The fact that I had something to do with building this company just makes you sick. The fact that I am the one that put this company on the map and helped you make it what it is today, that makes you sick to your stomach, brother.
McMahon: I think you're starting to believe in your own bullshit, Hogan. I could have anybody play the part of Hulk Hogan!
Hogan: If you actually think I was just the right guy at the right place at the right time, well then you're a bigger delusional bastard than I thought you were, McMahon.

The subtext here is enthralling. Most of what Vince said was based in fact, but the very core of the dispute—that Vince wanted Hogan gone—was disproven by Hulk's very existence in WWE. There's a thing in wrestling called a "worked shoot"—when somebody goes on microphone and says disparaging, real-life things that seem to veer off-script, when in fact the whole thing is staged for attention. It's a practice that became increasingly popular in the late '90s, and by this point it was almost impossible to have a feud between two people with a shared history that wasn't based on real-life grievance, or the manufactured perception thereof. With two people as intertwined as Hogan and McMahon, even in a manufactured world, reality was unavoidable.

Vince accused Hogan of disloyalty, of jumping ship when the money was better elsewhere. Hogan accused Vince of exploitation, of using his body and image until there was nothing left. The two agreed to a street fight at WrestleMania XIX, with Hogan's career on the line. On-screen, it was another longtime Hogan partner turning on him, only this time Hogan was completely in the right. When they staged the contract signing for the WrestleMania match, McMahon hit Hogan with a chair and left him bleeding, a subtle wink at Hogan-André all those years earlier.

When they got into the ring at WrestleMania, for the record, neither body had much left. It was slow, awkward, and drenched in blood, but it wasn't really about athletic competition. It was about dominance—about which man's version of history would stand unchallenged. The ending was unsatisfactory: Hogan won the street fight, but it hardly mattered; afterward, McMahon suspended him for the rest of his contract.

A month later, a new wrestler appeared, a masked man clad in red, white, and blue calling himself "Mr. America," who bore a striking resemblance to Hogan. (It was Hogan.) Determined to expose Hogan, McMahon fumed as the crowd giggled along. McMahon accused him of being a fraud—of hiding behind a mask, of stealing valor from the red-blooded American archetype he'd spent his career embodying.

The Mr. America angle wasn't subtle. Hogan was very obviously Hogan. The announcers knew it. The crowd knew it. Vince knew it. Hogan knew it. The storyline required everyone to pretend otherwise. This is pro wrestling in a nutshell: The pretense is the point. This is a time-honored wrestling trope, the suspended hero coming back under a mask (perhaps the best-known modern example was Dusty Rhodes masquerading as the Midnight Rider). Part of the act is that the heel is unable to prove beyond doubt that the masked man is the hero in question.

Masked men have always occupied a strange place in wrestling history. In Mexico, the mask is sacred—an identity more real than the face beneath it. In the United States, masks tend to function as disguises, symbols of shame, mystery, or reinvention. The masked wrestler is often someone trying to escape a past failure or to cheat the system that cast him aside. Mr. America fit neatly into that tradition. Hogan, "fired" by McMahon, returned under a mask to get revenge on the boss who had cast him out. But Hogan wasn't really hiding from Vince McMahon. He was hiding from himself.

By 2003, Hogan's mythology had become heavier than his body could comfortably carry. The immortal superhero of the 1980s had already died once, creatively, and been reborn as Hollywood Hogan in WCW. That turn was a confrontation with the audience. The Vince feud was something else. It was a confrontation with the man who had given Hogan the platform to become the Hulkster in the first place.

Their relationship was never just promoter and performer. It was symbiotic to the point of toxicity. McMahon needed Hogan as the face of his national expansion; Hogan needed McMahon's machine to turn charisma into empire. Each man believed—probably correctly—that the other owed him everything. And when WCW collapsed and Hogan returned to WWE, that unresolved debt hung in the air like fog.

Hogan won the WrestleMania match, but more important,

he survived. He endured. He refused to be erased. And yet, the Mr. America chapter complicates that reading. Hogan didn't simply defeat Vince McMahon and ride into the sunset. Instead, he retreated into absurdity. Lie detector tests. Courtroom sketches. Bad comedy. The mask became both shield and joke, a way to keep Hogan on television without forcing anyone—least of all Hogan—to fully reckon with what the feud had already exposed.

There's an argument that none of this was necessary. Hogan had already proven his relevance in 2002. He could have taken one last run against younger stars, soaked up the cheers, and left without ever standing across the ring from McMahon again. Plenty of legends have done exactly that. Just like his heel turn, the Vince feud risked diminishing Hogan, turning him into a punchline or, worse, a prop in someone else's vanity project. But wrestling careers don't end cleanly, especially not ones built on myth.

Hogan's entire persona was about finality—slam the giant, drop the leg, pose, leave nothing unresolved. To walk away without confronting Vince McMahon would have meant leaving the most significant relationship of his career in narrative limbo. WWE, under McMahon, had already made a habit of rewriting history to suit the present. By stepping into the ring with Vince, Hogan forced that history into the open, even if it came wrapped in farce.

Was it dignified? Not always. Was it coherent? Rarely. Was it revealing? Absolutely.

The feud acknowledged something wrestling usually prefers to bury: Power, not wins and losses, defines legacies. Hogan and McMahon weren't fighting over championships. They were fighting over authorship. But in the end, McMahon would always get the last word.

In June 2003, Hogan abruptly quit WWE in the middle of the storyline, unhappy with his role and the money he was making. Vince made this part of the story, naturally. He came into the ring the following week and showed video of Hogan putting on the Mr. America mask, and said he was fired, effective immediately. That was the end. In a feud that couldn't possibly have a fulfilling conclusion, reality managed to contrive the least fulfilling ending of all.

Hogan eventually returned for part-time appearances and sentimentality. I saw him make a surprise appearance at Madison Square Garden in 2005, and when his music hit, I was eight years old all over again. It's hard to convey the way these cues become ingrained, and how untethered from time so much of wrestling really is. One day we're litigating twenty years of history, and the next it's 1985 again. As a wrestling fan, you know the effect someone has had on you by the way you respond to their music, and I've never leapt out of my seat so quickly as I did for Hulk Hogan. He matters to me, to my childhood, and that is impossible to deny.

* * *

Hogan went on being Hogan until scandal made him an untenable guest star for WWE. McMahon continued to preside over WWE as its eternal antagonist, eventually eclipsed only by time and scandal of his own. But for a brief stretch in 2003, wrestling allowed itself to stage a confrontation between its two most important forces—and to admit, however clumsily, that its greatest hero and its greatest villain had always been reflections of each other.

The Mr. America mask came off eventually, as all masks do. What lingered was the acknowledgment that Hulk Hogan couldn't finish his in-ring career without looking Vince McMahon in the eye and saying, in the only language wrestling truly understands: This mattered, and it still does.

Whether Hogan needed that moment for his career is debatable. Whether wrestling needed it—whether it needed to see its past argue with itself in public—is harder to dismiss. In that sense, the feud wasn't just about closure. It was about admission. And in professional wrestling, that might be the most honest ending you can get.

CHAPTER 15

THE GHOST

HULK HOGAN VS. REALITY

The first time I met Hulk Hogan was at the ESPN Los Angeles office in 2011. My partner Peter Rosenberg and I were going to interview him for our podcast, and we were both excited. When we got word that Hogan was checking in at the front desk, I decided I had a minute to spare so I sprinted to the bathroom. When I exited the stall, there was Hulk Hogan, standing at the bathroom mirror, clipping his hair extensions in underneath his bandanna. I froze—this was not how I imagined meeting my childhood idol. Locked in a wistful stare-down with the mirror, Hulk didn't notice me, so I snuck out without him seeing me and without washing my hands.

When I officially met him minutes later, he looked at my "Hulkasized" T-shirt—a short-lived variation on Hulkamania that is almost entirely forgotten. "So you're the one who bought that," he said to me, immediately leaning into self-deprecation. We had researched every Hogan interview and made a list of questions that he had never been asked so that we could really make news with our interview, and it worked—we had him telling stories that no one had heard before. Then Hogan went on the rest of his media tour and told those same stories over and over again to anyone who would listen. When Hulk Hogan finds a routine that works, he replays it for every crowd.

This was postretirement Hulk Hogan, a likable and disarming PR machine. It was a huge moment for me as a lifelong wrestling fan, but I can hardly remember where we were sitting during the interview. The part I can never forget is the brief moment in the bathroom, the unnerving calm of a superhero putting on his mask, and the look in his eyes of sadness? Wariness? Exhaustion? I wonder about it to this day. The one thing I know is when he rounded the corner into the studio, he was Hulk Hogan, completely engaged, the legend in the flesh.

* * *

In the long arc of American wrestling fame, there are careers and then there are afterlives. Hulk Hogan has had several of both. The part everyone remembers—the red and yellow, the poses, the improbable biceps, the way he once felt less like a wrestler than like a federally mandated mascot—has been mythologized into something sturdy and nearly unkillable. But the story after the bell stopped ringing regularly is messier, stranger, and far more revealing than the cartoon heroics that made him famous. Hogan's post-wrestling life is not a victory lap. It's a prolonged echo, full of feedback and distortion, in which fame keeps showing up even after the reasons for it have curdled.

The thing about Hulk Hogan is that he was never just a wrestler. He was an idea that flexed. In the 1980s and early '90s, that idea was clean and simple: America with muscles, confidence without irony, vitamins as ideology. When that idea stopped fitting neatly into the culture, Hogan tried to keep reintroducing himself, in slightly altered forms, to an audience that kept changing faster than he did. His post-wrestling years are the record of that effort, and of what it costs to insist on staying visible when the spotlight has moved.

The other thing about Hulk Hogan is that he's, well, Hulk Hogan. Entirely. By the time he retired, there were no remnants of Terry Bollea left; the two men had become one and the same. It happens to all the greats—imagine a life of playing one role, on-screen and off-, and then imagine yourself trying to extricate yourself from it. Which is to say that Hogan's post-WWE career was not going to be different in any real way. It was just going to be unscripted, unmanaged, and performed outside of the arena that made him so automatically loved for so long. According to Bruce Prichard, in his WWF heyday, producers spent enormous amounts of time and money picking camera angles that obscured Hogan's bald spot. Hulk Hogan was about to enter a world in which he would be bald for all the world to see.

Hogan's first major post-WWE act, though, was still in the ring. Total Nonstop Action Wrestling, the upstart promotion that eventually branded itself as TNA, brought him in during 2010 with the promise—implicit and explicit—that he could help turn a scrappy alternative into a mainstream competitor. The idea was obvious: He had already done it once with WCW, and if anyone knew how to make wrestling feel big, it was Hogan. The problem was that TNA didn't need the Hulk Hogan of 2010; it needed a version of him that didn't exist.

His time in TNA was defined by contradictions. Hogan talked about elevating younger talent while positioning himself, again, at the center of the universe. He invoked innovation while leaning on familiar faces, old storylines, and the same gravitational pull he'd exerted for decades. For a while, the presence of Hogan and other veterans created a sense of legitimacy, or at least attention. But it also dragged the company into a kind of temporal confusion. TNA became a place where the past and present wrestled each other into a stalemate, with Hogan as the embodiment of both nostalgia and stagnation.

In his last matches there, Hogan could barely move, but unlike André at WrestleMania III, he didn't have a Hogan to carry him, and he certainly didn't have André's mystique—that had been squandered over the years. At the end, André could barely stand without a hand on the rope, yet he was out there trying. He was such a good performer that you hardly noticed it at the time; it's only in rewatching years later that the seams show. Hogan, on the other hand, was all seams in real time. As he did in the McMahon feud, he resorted to bleeding—a tried-and-true wrestling trope, but not in Hogan's repertoire during his heyday—to make the moments seem earned, even if they were in all truth empty.

If the wrestling didn't quite work, the branding did—at least in the short term. Hogan remained visible, quotable, and employable.

That visibility soon migrated to a different ring: reality television. *Hogan Knows Best* arrived in 2005, right as reality TV was refining its particular blend of intimacy and showbiz. It was a logical step: Reality television has much of the same kayfabe as pro wrestling did in the '80s; we know on some level that it's a put-on, but we engage with it as if it's real. The premise here was simple and faintly ridiculous: Hulk Hogan as overprotective dad, patriarch of a suburban Florida household, trying to keep his family safe while cameras documented everything he couldn't control.

The show worked because it leaned into Hogan's contradictions. He was both the indestructible hero and the anxious father, the man who once headlined WrestleMania now reduced to worrying about curfews and boyfriends. For viewers, that tension was the hook. For Hogan's family, it was something else entirely.

In hindsight, *Hogan Knows Best* feels like an extended stress test. The cameras didn't cause the fractures in Hogan's family, but they amplified them, reframed them, and made them harder to ignore. Privacy became a performance. Conflict became content. The show's success depended on blurring the line between the Hogans as people and the Hogans as characters, a line that had already been blurred by decades of wrestling mythology.

The effects were not subtle. Hogan's marriage to Linda deteriorated publicly, and their divorce played out with the same mix of spectacle and bitterness that defined so much of Hogan's public life. His children, Nick and Brooke, grew up on camera, their adolescence archived and replayed as entertainment. When real tragedy and scandal arrived—as it inevitably did—it didn't feel like a departure from the show so much as its darkest extension. Nick got into a wreck while speeding, and his passenger—his friend John

Graziano—suffered injuries that would leave him needing full-time medical care for the rest of his life. Nick was sentenced to eight months in jail. Brooke Hogan, the breakout star of the show, joined her dad as an on-screen character in TNA, but eventually stopped speaking to her parents.

❁ ❁ ❁

That brings us to the sex tape. Or, more accurately, to the moment when Hulk Hogan stopped being able to control the story of Hulk Hogan. In 2012, *Gawker* published a brief clip of a sex tape featuring Hogan and Heather Clem, then wife of radio personality (there's a conspicuous parallel to Savage and Miss Elizabeth in this) the Love Sponge. Hogan claimed he didn't know it was being recorded and sued *Gawker*, eventually winning $140 million from them and putting them out of business, despite reasonable claim that the piece was protected under the First Amendment. But during the trial, the full-length recording came out, and in it Hogan repeatedly used the n-word and said, "I am a racist, to a point."

The leaked tape, which became public in 2012, was more than a personal violation or a tabloid spectacle. It was a rupture. Hogan had spent his career carefully managing his image, even when that image shifted from superhero to reality-TV dad to elder statesman of wrestling. The tape ripped away the pretense that there was still a coherent character to protect. What emerged instead was a deeply uncomfortable portrait of a man whose private self collided violently with his public persona.

The legal battle ended with a decisive victory for Hogan and a dark, landmark moment in media law. But culturally, the win felt hollow. The tape, and the language captured within it, permanently altered how Hogan was perceived. He was no longer just a relic or a punchline; he was a problem. Humans have flaws, but the man who spent his life being more than human suddenly ran up against his inability to live up to his own expectations.

For a time, Hogan disappeared. WWE cut ties. Endorsements dried up. The silence that followed was an ambiguous exile; no one quite knew what to do with Hulk Hogan anymore, including Hogan himself. When he eventually resurfaced, it was with caution, and built on apologies and explanations that never quite landed cleanly. Redemption, in American celebrity culture, is often less about contrition than about endurance. Hogan had both time and a stubborn refusal to go away.

His return to WWE came in stages, beginning with a quiet reinstatement into the company's good graces and culminating in appearances meant to signal closure and forgiveness, or at least mutual benefit. That didn't go smoothly either. Upon his return, the roster gathered backstage to receive Hogan's apology for what he had said, but instead of saying "I'm sorry," he lectured them on avoiding hidden recording devices. Nonetheless, he was back; WWE has always understood the value of its legends, even the compromised ones. Hogan, for his part, finally needed WWE more than WWE needed him. The relationship had flipped.

If his WWE comeback represented something of a return to normalcy, Hogan's appearance at the 2024 Republican National Convention represented something else: a final attempt to anchor himself to a different kind of nostalgia. His speech leaned on the same themes that had powered his career—strength, patriotism, defiance—now repurposed for a political stage. It was an endorsement and also a brand alignment, Hogan positioning himself once again as a symbol of an America that existed more clearly in memory than in reality.

The reaction was predictably polarized. For some, it was a natural extension of the character Hogan had always played. For others, it felt like another misreading of the room, another instance of Hogan assuming that volume and certainty could substitute for relevance. 1980s Hulk Hogan was an American icon precisely because of his vagueness. He could be a hero for all because he stood, relatively speaking, for nothing. By choosing a side in a polarized America, he disappointed almost everybody.

Then there was January 6, 2025, the debut episode of *WWE Monday Night Raw* on Netflix. Hogan appeared, which was perhaps unsurprising for a legend of his wattage on such a momentous night. But he appeared not with an olive branch but rather to promote his new beer.

The crowd booed him viciously. This was not heel heat, not playful antagonism—just sustained, unmistakable rejection. It was one of the strangest sounds in wrestling: the audience turning on a man they once adored without question. Hogan tried to push through it, to deliver the familiar cadence and gestures, but the moment swallowed him. The boos weren't about a storyline. They were about memory, accountability, and a crowd that had grown up and moved on.

This underscores the central tension of Hulk Hogan's post-wrestling life: Hogan keeps showing up, but the contexts keep shifting in ways he doesn't fully grasp. What makes Hulk Hogan's last act compelling—and unsettling—is not that he fell from grace. It's that grace was never really the point. He would have been fine falling from grace. But he fell from relevance, and that left him permanently adrift. Hulk Hogan mattered until the moment he didn't.

Hogan's fame was built on excess, on a willingness to take up space and dare anyone to look away. When the culture changed, that instinct didn't. The platforms did as well. Wrestling became smaller. Reality TV became harsher. Politics became another arena for performance.

Through it all, Hogan has remained fundamentally the same: a man convinced that if he kept talking, posing, and reasserting his presence, the world will eventually meet him where he stands. Sometimes it does. Often, it doesn't.

There's a temptation to frame Hogan's story as a cautionary tale, but that feels too tidy. Certainly there's a "never meet your heroes" lesson at the core of this, and a lesson for Hogan, who lived his life on display to the point that he practically invited everyone into the darkest corners of his person. But the deeper meaning is messier than that, and more American. Hulk Hogan is what happens when a pop-culture avatar outlives the conditions that made him legible. He's a reminder that fame can diminish, but you are never really free of its burden. And once you've been that hot, that bright, you spend the rest of your life chasing the feeling, even as the audience learns how to boo.

In the end, Hogan's post-wrestling life isn't strictly about redemption or downfall. It's about narcissism, the awkward sin of insistence. The ring got smaller, then disappeared, but the performance never really stopped. The difference is that now, the cheers are conditional, the boos are real, and the myth no longer does the heavy lifting.

ACKNOWLEDGMENTS

Thanks to Bill Simmons, Sean Fennessey, and everyone at *The Ringer* for making my childhood fascination a real job. Thanks to Bryan Curtis for watching alongside me all those years, and for suggesting this book. Thanks to Anthony Mattero and Sean Desmond for making it a reality.

Thanks to my parents, as I always say, for not making me turn off this trash when I was a kid, and to my wife and kids for not making me turn it off as an adult. And specifically to my father, who took me to the Louisville Gardens to see Hogan face off against Killer Khan. Hogan inexplicably wrestled in the middle of the card, and when I asked my dad why, he said, "He probably has a plane to catch." So I guess I should say thanks to Hulk Hogan for fitting us into his schedule.

ABOUT THE AUTHOR

David Shoemaker has been writing about wrestling since 2009. He is the host of the podcast *The Masked Man Show with Kaz*, a writer at *The Ringer*, and the author of *The Squared Circle: Life, Death, and Professional Wrestling.*